The Mother at Home

Raising Your Children in the Fear of the Lord

John S.C. Abbott

SOLID GROUND CHRISTIAN BOOKS
Birmingham, Alabama USA

SOLID GROUND CHRISTIAN BOOKS
2090 Columbiana Rd., Suite 2000
Birmingham, AL 35216
(205) 443-0311
sgcb@charter.net
http://solid-ground-books.com

THE MOTHER AT HOME:
Raising Your Children in the Fear of the Lord

by John S.C. Abbott (1805-1877)

First published in 1833 by The American Tract Society, NY City, NY

SGCB Classic Reprints

ISBN: 1-932474-70-6

Cover Design by Borgo Design, Tuscaloosa, Alabama
Contact them by e-mail at nelbrown@comcast.net

Cover image from the first edition of this book, published by the
American Tract Society.

Manufactured in the United States of America

The Author's Dedication

TO MY MOTHER AND FATHER

This book is most affectionately dedicated. For the principles here inculcated, I am indebted to the instructions I received, and the scenes I witnessed, at your fire-side. That God may render them available, in conferring the same joy upon other families, which they have so richly shed upon yours, is the prayer of your

GRATEFUL SON

The Author's Preface

The object of this book is *practical utility,* not literary effect. It was written for mothers in the common walks of life. There are many mothers, in every village of our land, who are looking eagerly for information respecting the government of their children. It is hoped that the following treatise may render them some assistance.

Some persons may object to the minuteness of detail, and the familiarity of illustrations, occasionally introduced. We, however, are persuaded that this objection will not be made by the *mothers.* Education consists in attention to *little things.*

The religious sentiments inculcated in this book are those usually denominated *evangelical.* We have proceeded upon the principle that here is the commencement of eternal existence, and that the great object of education is to prepare the child for its heavenly home.

When a person writes upon the subject of family government, the first thought which arises in the minds of many readers, is, "we will see how he succeeds in his own family." There are many motives, such as indolence, false tenderness, etc. operating to induce a parent to neglect known duty. The principles contained in this book may be correct, even though the author should fail to enforce them.

This treatise was commenced with particular reference to the mothers who attend my ministry. That it may be of assistance to them, in their efforts to lead their children to the Savior, is the earnest prayer of their friend and pastor,

John S.C. Abbott
Worcester, MA
March 1833

TABLE OF CONTENTS

CHAPTER ONE

RESPONSIBILITY. –Anecdote. The Mother of Washington. Lord Byron. John Newton. The Sailor. Consequences of a daughter's sin. The Maniac. The way to avoid maternal anguish. . . . . .Page 1

CHAPTER TWO

MATERNAL AUTHORITY: Part One.— Necessity of obedience. What is meant by obedience. The sick child. The way to obtain obedience. Scene in a farm house. Instance of maternal faithfulness. Mothers' excuses. Two family scenes. A mother's power. . . .Page 13

CHAPTER THREE

MATERNAL AUTHORITY: Part Two – Contests with children. Anecdote. The way to avoid contests. Variations of feeling. Difference of natural disposition. Variations of punishment. Unjust punishment. Illustrations. Time to commence government. Effects of severity upon the children. . . . . Page 27

CHAPTER FOUR

THE MOTHER'S DIFFICULTIES – Necessity of self-control. Illustration. Necessity of resolution. The unhappy widow. Anecdote of Bonaparte. Fatal Indulgence of sick children. Importance of harmony of views between both parents. Family saved from ruin by a faithful and judicious mother. . . . . Page 47

CHAPTER FIVE

FAULTS AND ERRORS – Talking about children in their presence. Anecdote. Self-conceit, how produced. Injudicious remarks of visitors. The vain child. Making exhibitions of children's attainments. Repeating hymns. Remarks of an English gentleman. Secluding children from society. A family scene. Loquacity. Anecdote. Deceiving children. The Physician. Good effects of approbation. Basil Hall. Imaginary fears. Appalling consequences of resorting to them for punishment. . . . . Page 63

CHAPTER SIX

RELIGIOUS INSTRUCTION: Part One – A mother's influence. Importance of deep devotional feeling. Dying scene. The cheerful aspect in which religion should be presented. Appropriate occasions for religious instruction. Tenderness of feeling. The storm. Sickness. The death of a child. Anecdote. The summer's morning. Loss of a ball. The gentleman and the cabin-boy. Inappropriate occasions. Excitement. Tedious conversation. . . . . Page 85

CHAPTER SEVEN

RELIGIOUS INSTRUCTION: Part Two – Indefinite views of heaven. Vivid description of the inspired writers. Intellectual delight. Rapture of melody. Joy of friendship. Beauty of scenery. The Savior. Impression a Savior's love produces on the mind of a child. Nathan Dickerman. Prayer with children. The gambler. English gentleman. Teaching children to pray. Mode. Anecdote. Expect success. Sources of encouragement. Evil consequences of giving publicity to the hopeful piety of a child. . . . . Page 101

CHAPTER EIGHT

RESULTS – A mother's joys. A mother's influence on future generations. Consequences of a father's neglect of duty. Necessity of studying the subject of Education. Consequences of ignorance. Keeping journals. Extracts from a mother's note-book. Cessation of toil, and a heavenly home. . . . . Page 119

"My mother was the most beautiful woman I ever saw. All I am I owe to my mother. I attribute all my success in life to the moral, intellectual and physical education I received from her."
– George Washington

"I remember my mother's prayers and they have always followed me. They have clung to me all my life. All that I am or ever hope to be, I owe to my angel Mother."
– Abraham Lincoln

"A mother is the truest friend we have, when trials, heavy and sudden, fall upon us; when adversity takes the place of prosperity; when friends who rejoice with us in our sunshine, desert us; when troubles thicken around us, still will she cling to us, and endeavor by her kind precepts and counsels to dissipate the clouds of darkness, and cause peace to return to our hearts."
– Washington Irving

"Even He that died for us upon the cross, in the last hour, in the unutterable agony of death, was mindful of His mother, as if to teach us that this holy love should be our last worldly thought–the last point of earth from which the soul should take its flight for heaven."
– Henry Wadsworth Longfellow

CHAPTER ONE

Responsibility

A few years ago, some gentlemen who were associated in preparing for the ministry, felt interested in ascertaining what proportion of their number had pious mothers. They were greatly surprised and delighted in finding that out of one hundred and twenty students, over a hundred had been borne by a mother's prayers, and directed by a mother's counsels, to the Savior. Though some of these had broken away from all the restraints of home, and like the prodigal, had wandered in sin and sorrow, yet they could not forget the impressions of childhood, and were eventually brought to the Savior, to be a mother's joy and blessing. Many interesting facts have, within a few years, drawn the attention of Christians to this subject. The efforts which a mother makes for the improvement of her child in knowledge and virtue are necessarily retired and unobtrusive. The world knows not of them; and hence the world has been slow to perceive how powerful and extensive this secret and silent influence is. But circumstances are now directing the eyes of the community to the nursery, and the truth is daily coming more distinctly before the public; that the influence which is exerted upon the mind during the first eight or ten years of

1

existence, in a great degree guides the destinies of that mind for time and eternity. And as the mother is the guardian and guide of the early years of life, from her goes the most powerful influence in the formation of the character of man. And why should it not be so? What impressions can be more strong, and more lasting, than those received upon the mind in the freshness and the susceptibility of youth? What instructor can gain greater confidence and respect than a mother? And where can there be delight in acquiring knowledge, if not when the little flock cluster around a mother's knee to hear of God and heaven?

"A good boy generally makes a good man." Said the mother of Washington, "George was always a good boy." Here we see one secret of his greatness. George Washington had a mother who made him a good boy, and instilled into his heart those principles which raised him to be the benefactor of his country, and one of the brightest ornaments of the world. The mother of Washington is entitled to a nation's gratitude. She taught her boy the principles of obedience, and moral courage, and virtue. She, in a great measure, formed the character of the hero, and the statesman. It was by her own fireside that she taught her playful boy to govern himself; and thus was he prepared for the brilliant career of usefulness which he afterward pursued. We are indebted to God for the gift of Washington; but we are no less indebted to him for the gift of his inestimable mother. Had she been a weak, and indulgent, and unfaithful parent, the unchecked energies of Washington might have elevated him to the throne of a tyrant; or youthful disobedience might have prepared the way for a life of crime and a dishonored grave.

2

Chapter One — Responsibility

Byron[1] had a mother just the reverse of Lady Washington; and the character of the mother was transferred to the son. We cannot wonder then at his character and conduct, for we seé them to be the almost necessary consequence of the education he received, and the scenes witnessed in his mother's parlor. She would at one time allow him to disobey with impunity; again she would fly into a rage and beat him. She thus taught him to defy all authority, human and divine; to indulge, without restraint, in sin; to give himself up to the power of every maddening passion. It was the mother of Byron who laid the foundation of his pre-eminence in guilt. She taught him to plunge into that sea of profligacy and wretchedness, upon whose agitated waves he was tossed for life. If the crimes of the poet deserve the execration of the world—the world cannot forget that it was the mother who fostered in his youthful heart those passions which made the son a curse to his fellowmen.

There are, it is true, innumerable causes incessantly operating in the formation of character. A mother's influence is by no means the only influence which is exerted. Still it may be the most powerful; for, with God's ordinary blessing, it may form in the youthful mind the habits, and implant the principles, to which other influences are to give permanency and vigor.

A pious and faithful mother may have a dissolute child. He may break away from all restraints, and God may leave him to "eat the fruit of his own devices." The parent, thus afflicted and brokenhearted, can only bow before the sovereignty of her

---

[1]Lord Byron (1788-1824), world-renown poet, was born on 22 January 1788. His mother Catherine came from the lawless line of Scottish Gordons, and his father, John Byron, of even worse reputation, had run through his wife's fortune and was hiding in France, and later died a drunkard, turning his title over to his son.

Maker, who says, "be still, and know that I am God."[2] The consciousness, however, of having done one's duty, divests this affliction of much of its bitterness. And beside, such cases are rare. Profligate children are generally the offspring of parents who have neglected the moral and religious education of their family. Some parents are themselves profligate, and thus not only allow their children to grow up unrestrained, but by their example lure them to sin. But there are others, who are very upright, and virtuous and even pious themselves, who do, nevertheless, neglect the moral culture of their children; and as a consequence, they grow up in disobedience and sin. It matters but little what the cause is which leads to this neglect. The neglect itself will ordinarily be followed by disobedience and self-will.

Hence the reason that children of eminent men, both in church and state, are not infrequently the disgrace of their parents. If the mother is unaccustomed to govern her children, if she look to the father to enforce the obedience, and to control; when *he* is absent, all family government is absent, and the children are left to run wild; to learn lessons of disobedience; to practice arts of deception; to build upon the foundation of contempt for a mother, a character of insubordination and iniquity. But if the children are under the efficient government of a judicious mother, the reverse of this is almost invariably the case. And since, in nearly every instance, the early years of life are entrusted to a mother's care, it follows that maternal influence, more than any thing else, forms the future character.

---

[2] Psalm 46:10.

Chapter One — Responsibility

The history of John Newton[3] is often mentioned as a proof of the deep and lasting impression which a mother may produce upon the mind of her child. He had a pious mother. She often retired to her closet, and placing her hand upon his youthful head, implored God's blessing upon her boy. These prayers and instructions sunk deep into his heart. He could not but revere that mother. He could not but feel that there was a holiness in such a character, demanding reverence and love. He could not tear from his heart, in after life, the impressions then produced. Though he became a wicked wanderer, though he forsook friends and home, and every virtue; the remembrance of a mother's prayers, like a guardian angel, followed him wherever he went. He mingled in the most dissipated and disgraceful scenes of a sailor's life, and while surrounded with guilty associates, in midnight revelry, he would fancy he felt the soft hand of his mother upon his head, pleading with God to forgive and bless her boy. He went to the coast of Africa, and became even more degraded than the savages upon her dreary shores. But the soft hand of his mother was still upon his head, and the fervent prayers of his mother still thrilled in his heart. And this influence, after the lapse of many guilty years, brought back the prodigal, a penitent and a child of God; elevated him to be one of the brightest ornaments of the Christian church, and to guide many sons and daughters to glory. What a forcible comment is this upon the power of maternal influence! And what encouragement does this present to every mother to be faithful in her efforts to train up her child for God! Had Mrs.

---

[3] John Newton (1725-1807) is perhaps best known for his hymn *Amazing Grace*, but he wrote dozens of other hymns and numerous volumes of other works from his pen and heart. *Banner of Truth* has reprinted this 6 volume set.

Newton neglected her duty, had she even been as remiss as many Christian mothers, her son, to all human view, might have continued in sin, and been an outcast from heaven. It was through the influence of the mother that the son was saved. Newton became afterward a most successful preacher of the Gospel, and every soul which he was instrumental in saving, as he sings the song of redeeming mercy, will, through eternity, bless God that Newton had such a mother.

The influence thus exerted upon the mind, in early childhood, may, for many years, be apparently lost. When a son leaves home, and enters upon the busy world, many are the temptations which come crowding upon him. If he leaves not his mother with established principles of religion and self-control, he will most assuredly fall before these temptations. He may indeed fall, even after all a mother has done, or can do; and he may become deeply involved in guilt. But he may apparently forget every lesson he learnt at home, while the influence of a mother's instructions, and a mother's prayers, is yet working powerfully and *effectually* in his heart. He will think of a mother's tears, when remorse keeps him awake at midnight, or when danger threatens him with speedy arraignment at the bar of God. The thoughts of the sacredness of home will often throw bitterness into his cup of guilty pleasure, and compel him to sigh for the virtue and the peace he has forsaken. Even though far away, in abodes of infamy, degraded and abandoned, he must occasionally think of a brokenhearted mother. Thus may he, after many years, perhaps long after she has gone down to the grave, be led, by the remembrance of her virtues, to forsake his sins.

Chapter One — Responsibility

A short time ago, a gentleman, in one of our most populous cities, was going to attend a seaman's meeting in the mariner's chapel. Directly opposite the chapel there was a sailor's boarding house. In the doorway sat a hardy, weather-beaten sailor, with arms folded, and puffing a cigar, watching the people as they gradually assembled for the meeting. The gentleman walked up to him and said, "Well, my friend, won't you go with us to meeting?" "No!" said the sailor, bluntly. The gentleman, who, from the appearance of the man, was prepared for a repulse mildly replied, "You look, my friend, as though you had seen hard days; have you a mother?" The sailor raised his head, looked earnestly in the gentleman's face, and made no reply.

The gentleman continued: "Suppose your mother was here now, what advice would she give you?" The tears rushed into the eyes of the poor sailor; he tried for a moment to conceal them, but could not; and, hastily brushing them away with the back of his rough hand, rose and said, with a voice almost inarticulate through emotion, "I'll go to the meeting." He crossed the street, entered the door of the chapel, and took his seat with the assembled congregation.

What afterward became of the man is not known. It is however almost certain that he must have had a mother who had given him good instruction; and when the gentleman appealed to her, hardened as the sailor was, his heart melted. It is by no means improbable that this interview may have checked this man in his sins, and led him to Christ. At any event, it shows the strength of maternal influence. It shows that years of wandering and of sin cannot erase from the heart the impression which a mother's instructions and a mother's prayers have left there.

It is a great trial to have children undutiful when young but it is a tenfold greater affliction to have a child grow up to maturity in disobedience, and become a dissolute and abandoned man. How many parents have passed days of sorrow and nights of sleeplessness in consequence of the misconduct of their offspring! How many have had their hearts broken, and their gray hairs brought down with sorrow to the grave, solely in consequence of their own neglect to train up their children in the nurture and admonition of the Lord! Your future happiness is in the hands of your children. They may throw gloom over all your prospects, embitter every enjoyment, and make you so miserable, that your only prospect of relief will be in death.

That little girl whom you now fondle upon your knee, and who plays, so full of enjoyment, upon your floor, has entered a world where temptations are thick around. What is to enable her to resist these temptations, but established principles of piety? And where is she to obtain these principles, but from a mother's instructions and example? If, through your neglect now, she should hereafter yield herself to temptation and sin, what must become of your peace of mind? O mother! Little are you aware of the wretchedness with which your loved daughter may hereafter overwhelm you!

Many illustrations of the most affecting nature might be here introduced. It would be easy to appeal to a vast number of living sufferers, in attestation of the woe which the sin of the child has occasioned. You may go, not only in imagination, but in reality, to the darkened chamber, where the mother sits weeping, and refusing to be comforted, for a daughter is lost to virtue and to heaven. Still, no person can imagine how

8

overwhelming the agony which must prey upon a mother thus dishonored and brokenhearted. This is a sorrow which can only be understood by one who has tasted its bitterness and felt its weight. We may go to the house of piety and prayer, and find the father and mother with countenances emaciated with suffering; not a smile plays upon their features, and the mournful accents of their voice tell how deeply seated is their sorrow. Shall we inquire into the cause of this heart-rending grief? The mother would only reply with tears and sobs. The father would summon all his fortitude, and say, "my daughter"—and say no more. The anguish of his spirit would prevent the farther utterance of his grief.

Is this exaggeration? No! Let your lovely daughter, now your pride and joy, be abandoned to infamy, be an outcast from society, and you must feel what language cannot express.

This is a dreadful subject; but it is one which the mother must feel and understand. There are facts which might here be introduced, sufficient to make every parent tremble. We might lead you to the dwelling of the clergyman, and tell you that a daughter's sin has murdered the mother, and sent paleness to the cheek, and trembling to the frame, and agony to the heart of the aged father. We might carry you to the parlor of the rich man, and show you all the elegance and the opulence with which he is surrounded; and yet he would tell you that he was one of the most unhappy of the sons of affliction, and that he would gladly give all his treasures if he could purchase back a daughter's virtue; that he could gladly lie down to die, if he could thus blot out the remembrance of a daughter's infamy.

No matter what your situation in life may be, that little child, now so innocent, whose playful endearments and happy laugh awaken such thrilling emotions in your heart, may cause you years of most unalleviated misery.

And mother! Look at that drunken vagrant, staggering by your door. Listen to his horrid imprecations, as bloated and ragged he passes along. That wretch has a mother. Perhaps, widowed and in poverty, she needs the comfort and support of an affectionate son. You have a son. You *may* soon be a widow. If your son is dissolute, you are doubly widowed; you are worse, infinitely worse than childless. You cannot now endure even the thought that your son will ever be thus abandoned. How dreadful then must be the experience of the reality!

I once knew a mother who had an only son. She loved him most ardently, and could not bear to deny him any indulgence. He, of course, soon learned to rule his mother. At the death of his father, the poor woman was left at the mercy of this vile boy. She had neglected her duty when he was young, and now his ungovernable passions had become too strong for her control. Self-willed, turbulent, and revengeful, he was his mother's bitterest curse. His paroxysms of rage at times amounted almost to madness. One day, infuriated with his mother, he set fire to her house, and it was burned to the ground, with all its contents, and she was left in the extremist state of poverty. He was imprisoned as an incendiary,[4] and, in his cell, he became a maniac, if he was not such before, and madly dug out his own eyes. He now lays in perpetual darkness, confined by the stone walls and grated bars of his dungeon, an infuriated madman.

O how hard it must be for a mother, after all her pain, and anxiety, and watchings, to find her son a demoniac spirit,

---

[4] Any person who maliciously sets fire to a building or other valuable property.

instead of a guardian and friend! You have watched over your child, through all the months of its helpless infancy. You have denied yourself, that you might give it comfort. When it has been sick, you have been unmindful of your own weariness, and your own weakness, and the livelong night you have watched at its cradle, administering to all its wants. When it has smiled, you have felt a joy which none but a parent can feel, and have pressed your much loved treasure to your bosom, praying that its future years of obedience and affection might be your ample reward. And now, how dreadful a requital, for that child to grow up to hate and abuse you; to leave you friendless, in sickness and in poverty; to squander all his earnings in haunts of iniquity and degradation.

How entirely is your earthly happiness at the disposal of your child! His character is now, in an important sense, in your hands, and you are to form it for good or for evil. If you are consistent in your government, and faithful in the discharge of your duties, your child will probably through life revere you, and be the stay and solace of your declining years. If, on the other hand, you cannot summon resolution to punish your child when disobedient; if you do not curb his passions; if you do not bring him to entire and willing subjection to your authority; you must expect that he will be your curse. In all probability, he will despise you for your weakness. Unaccustomed to restraints at home, he will break away from all restraints, and make you wretched by his life, and disgraceful in his death.

But few parents think of this as they ought. They are not conscious of the tremendous consequences dependent upon the efficient and decisive government of their children.

11

Thousands of parents now stand in our land like oaks blighted and scathed by lightning and storms. Thousands have had every hope wrecked, every prospect darkened, and have become the victims of the most agonizing and heart-rending disappointment, solely in consequence of the misconduct of their children. And yet thousands of others are going on in the same way, preparing to experience the same suffering, and are apparently unconscious of their danger.

It is true that there are many mothers who feel their responsibilities perhaps as deeply as it is best they should feel them. But there are many others—even of Christian mothers—who seem to forget that their children will ever be less under their control than they are while young. And they are training them up, by indecision and indulgence, soon to tyrannize over their parents with a rod of iron—and to pierce their hearts with many sorrows. If you are unfaithful to your child when he is young, he will be unfaithful to you when be is old. If you indulge him in all his foolish and unreasonable wishes when he is a child, when he becomes a man he will indulge himself; he will gratify every desire of his heart; and your sufferings will be rendered the more poignant by the reflection that it was your own unfaithfulness which has caused your ruin. If you would be the happy mother of a happy child, give your attention, and your efforts, and your prayers, to the great duty of training him up for God and heaven.

CHAPTER TWO

Maternal Authority: Part I

I have thus endeavored to show the mother how much her happiness is dependant upon the good or bad character of her children. Your own reflections and observation have, doubtless, impressed this subject most deeply upon your heart. The question has probably often presented itself to your mind, while reading the previous chapter, "How shall I govern my children, so as to secure their virtue and happiness?" This question I shall now endeavor to answer:

I. *Obedience* is absolutely essential to proper family government. Without this, all other efforts will be in vain. You may pray with, and for your children; you may strive to instruct them in religious truth; you may be unwearied in your efforts to make them happy, and to gain their affection. But if they are in habits of disobedience, your instructions will be lost, and your toil in vain. And by *obedience,* I do not mean languid and dilatory yielding to repeated threats, but prompt and cheerful acquiescence in parental commands. Neither is it enough that a child should yield to your *arguments* and *persuasions.* It is essential that he should submit to your authority.

I will suppose a case in illustration of this last remark. Your little daughter is sick; you go to her with the medicine which has been prescribed for her, and the following dialogue ensues.

"Here, my daughter is some medicine for you."

"I don't want to take it, mamma."

"Yes, my dear, do take it, for it will make you feel better."

"No it won't, mother; I don't want it."

"Yes it will, my child; the doctor says it will."

"Well, it don't taste good, and I don't want it."

The mother continues her persuasions, and the child persists in its refusal. After a long and wearisome conflict, the mother is compelled either to throw the medicine away, or to resort to compulsion, and force down the unpalatable drug. Thus, instead of appealing to her own supreme authority, she is appealing to the *reason of the child,* and, under these circumstances, the child of course refuses to submit.

A mother, not long ago, under similar circumstances, not being able to persuade her child to take the medicine, and not having sufficient resolution to compel it, threw the medicine away. When the physician next called, she was ashamed to acknowledge her lack of government, and therefore did not tell him that the medicine had not been given. The physician finding the child worse left another prescription, supposing the previous one had been properly administered. But the child had no idea of being convinced of the propriety of taking the nauseous dose, and the renewed efforts of the mother were unavailing. Again the fond and foolish, but cruel parent threw the medicine away, and the fever was left to rage unchecked in its veins. Again the physician called, and was surprised to find the inefficacy of his prescriptions, and that the poor little sufferer was at the verge of death. The mother, when informed that her child must die, was in an agony, and confessed what she had done. But it was too late. The child died. And think you that mother gazed upon its pale corpse with any *common* emotions of anguish? Think you the idea never entered her mind that she was the destroyer of her child? Physicians will tell you that many children have been thus lost. Unaccustomed to obedience when well, they were still more averse to it when sick. The efforts which are made to induce a stubborn child to take medicine often produce such an excitement as entirely to counteract the effect of the prescription; and thus is a mother often called to weep over the grave of her child, simply because she has not taught that child to obey.

It is certainly the duty of parents to convince their children of the reasonableness and propriety of their requirements. This should be done to instruct them, and to make them acquainted with moral obligation. But there should always be *authority* sufficient to enforce prompt obedience, whether the child can see the reason of the requirement or not. Indeed, it is impossible to govern a child by mere argument. Many cases must occur, in which it will be incapable of seeing the reasonableness of the command; and often its wishes will be so strongly opposed to duty, that all the efforts to convince will be in vain.

The first thing therefore to be aimed at, is to bring your child under perfect subjection. Teach him that he must obey you. Sometimes give him your reasons; again withhold them.

But let him perfectly understand that he is to do as he is bid. Accustom him to immediate and cheerful acquiescence in your will. This is obedience. And this is absolutely essential to good family government. Without this, your family will present one continued scene of noise and confusion; the toil of rearing up your children will be almost insupportable, and, in all probability, your heart will be broken by their future licentiousness or ingratitude.

II. We come now to the inquiry, *how is this habit of obedience to be established?* This is not so difficult a matter as many imagine. It does not require profound learning, or a mysterious skill, which pertains but to the few. Where do you find the best regulated families? Are they in the houses of the rich? Do the children of our most eminent men furnish the best patterns for imitation? Obviously not. In some of the most humble dwellings we find the beautiful spectacle of an orderly and well regulated family. On the other hand, in the mansions of the wealthiest or most eminent men of our country, we may often find a family of rude girls and ungovernable boys,—a picture of wild misrule. It is not greatness of talent, or profound learning, which is requisite to teach a child obedience. The principles by which we are to be guided are very simple and very plain.

Never give a command which you do not intend shall be obeyed. There is no more effectual way of teaching a child disobedience, than by giving commands which you have no intention of enforcing. A child is thus habituated to disregard its mother; and in a short time the habit becomes so strong, and the child's contempt for the mother so confirmed, that entreaties and threats are alike unheeded.

"Mary, let that book alone," says a mother to her little daughter, who is trying to pull the Bible from the table.

Mary stops for a moment, and then takes hold of the book again.

Pretty soon the mother looks up and sees that Mary is still playing with the Bible. "Did not you hear me tell you to let that book alone?" she exclaims: "Why don't you obey?"

Mary takes away her hand for a moment, but is soon again at her forbidden amusement. By and by, down comes the Bible upon the floor. Up jumps the mother, and hastily giving the child a passionate blow, exclaims, "There then, obey me next time." The child screams, and the mother picks up the Bible, saying, "I wonder why my children do not obey me better."

This is not a very interesting family scene, but every one of my readers will admit that it is not an uncommon one. And is it strange that a child, thus managed, should be disobedient? No. She is actually led on by her mother to insubordination; she is actually *taught* to pay no heed to her directions. Even the improper punishment which sometimes follows transgression is not inflicted on account of her disobedience, but for the accidental consequences. In the case above described, had the Bible not fallen, the disobedience of the child would have passed unpunished. Let it be an immutable principle in family government, that your word is law.

I was once, when riding in the country, overtaken by a shower, and compelled to seek shelter in a farm house. Half a dozen rude and ungovernable boys were racing about the room, in such an uproar as to prevent the possibility of conversation with the father, who was sitting by the fire. As I, however, endeavored to make some remark, the father shouted out, "Stop that noise, boys."

17

They paid no more heed to him than they did to the rain. Soon again, in an irritated voice, he exclaimed,

"Boys, be still, or I will whip you; as sure as you are alive I will." But the boys, as though accustomed to such threats, screamed and quarreled without intermission.

At last the father said to me, "I believe I have got the worst boys in town; I never can make them mind me."

The fact was, these boys had the worst *father* in town. He was teaching them disobedience as directly and efficiently as he could. He was giving commands which he had no intention of enforcing, and they knew it. This, to be sure, is an extreme case. But just so far as any mother allows her authority to be disregarded, so far does she expose herself to the contempt of her children, and actually teaches them lessons of disobedience.

And is there any difficulty in enforcing obedience to any definite command? Take the case of the child playing with the Bible. A mild and judicious mother says distinctly and decidedly to her child, "My daughter, that is the Bible, and you must not touch it." The child hesitates for a moment, but yielding to the strong temptation, is soon playing with the forbidden book. The mother immediately rises, takes the child, and carries her into her chamber. She sits down and says calmly, "Mary, I told you not to touch the Bible, and you have disobeyed me. I am very sorry, for now I must punish you."

Mary begins to cry, and to promise not to do so again.

"But Mary," says the mother, "you have disobeyed me, and you must be punished."

Mary continues to cry, but the mother seriously and calmly punishes her. She inflicts real pain—pain that will be remembered.

18

The mother, soon seeing how he is wearing the carpet and bruising the furniture, gets up, gives Charles a shake, and places the tongs in their proper place; but by the time she is fairly seated, and at her work again, Charles is astride the shovel, and traveling at the top of his speed.

I need not continue this picture. But every one knows that it is not exaggerated. Such scenes do often occur. Thousands of immortal spirits are trained up in this turbulence, and anarchy, and noise, for time and for eternity. Now this mother will tell you that she *has not time* to bring her children into subjection. Whereas, had she been faithful with each individual child, she would have saved herself an immense amount of time and toil.

We will suppose the case of another mother, who has the same work to perform. She has taught her children prompt and implicit obedience. She gives three of them perhaps some blocks, in one corner of the room, and tells them that they may play *"build houses,"* but that they must not make much noise, and must not interrupt her, for she wishes to be busy. The other three she places in another corner of the room, with their slates, and tells them that they may play *"make pictures."* The children, accustomed to such orderly arrangements, employ themselves very quietly and happily for perhaps three quarters of an hour. The mother goes on uninterrupted in her work. Occasionally she raises her eyes and says an encouraging word to her children, now noticing the little architects in the corner, and now glancing her eye at the drawings upon the slates; thus showing the children that she sympathizes with them, and takes an interest in their enjoyments. The children are pleased and happy. The mother is undisturbed.

21

She does not let them continue their amusements till they are weary of them. But after they have played perhaps three quarters of an hour, she says,

"Come, children, you have played long enough; you may take up all your little blocks and put them away in the drawer."

"O, mother," says Maria, "do let me play a little while longer, for I have got my house almost done."

"Well, you may finish it," says the judiciously kind mother, "but tell me as soon as it is done."

In a few minutes Maria says, "There, mamma, see what a large house I have built!" The mother looks at it, and adds a pleasant word of encouragement, and then tells them to put all their blocks in the proper place. She tells the children with the slates to hang them up, and to put away their pencils; so that, the next day, when slates and blocks are wanted, no time may be lost in searching for them.

Now which mother has *the most time?* and which, mother has the *happiest* time? And which mother will find the most comfort in the subsequent character and affection of her children?

Perhaps some one will say, this is a pleasing picture; but where are we to look for its reality? It is indeed to be regretted that such scenes are of so infrequent occurrence. But it is far from being true that they do not occur. There are many such families of happy parents and affectionate children. And these families are not confined to the wealthy and the learned. It requires not wealth, and it requires not extensive learning, to train up such a family. The principle of government is simple and plain. It is to begin with enforcing obedience to every command. It is to establish the principle that a mother's word is never to be disregarded. Every judicious parent will, indeed, try to gratify her children in their reasonable wishes. She will study to make them happy; but she will never allow them to gratify themselves in contradiction to her wishes.

To illustrate this, let us refer to the children playing with the blocks. The mother tells them to put up the blocks. Maria asks permission to play a few moments longer, till she can finish her house. The mother, desirous of making her children as happy as she can, grants this reasonable wish. Here is a judicious indulgence. But suppose again that the children had continued playing without regard to their mother's command. They intend perhaps to continue their amusement only till they complete the pile then in progress. Here is an act of direct disobedience. The children are consulting their own inclinations instead of the commands of their mother. A judicious parent will not allow such an act to pass unnoticed or unpunished. She may perhaps think, considering the circumstances of the case, that a serious reprimand is all that is required. But she will not fail to seize upon the occasion to instill into their minds a lesson of obedience.

Is it said that by noticing such *little things* a mother must be continually finding fault? But it is not *a little thing* for a child to disobey a mother's commands. This one act of disregarding authority prepares the way for another. It is the commencement of evil which must be resisted. The very first appearances of insubordination must be checked. There are doubtless cases of trifling faults occurring, which a wise parent will judge it expedient to overlook. Children will be thoughtless and inadvertent. They will occasionally err from strict propriety, without any real intention of doing wrong. Judgment is here requisite in deciding what things must he overlooked; but we may be assured, I think, that direct and open disobedience is not, in any case, to be classed among the number of trifling faults. The eating of an apple banished our first parents from paradise. The atrocity of the offence consisted in its *disobedience* of a divine command.

Now, every mother has *power* to obtain prompt obedience, if she commences with her children when they are young. They are then entirely in her hands. All their enjoyments are at her disposal. God has thus given her all the power she needs to govern and guide them as she pleases. We have endeavored to show, by the preceding illustrations, that the fundamental principle of government is, *when you do give a command, invariably enforce its obedience.* And God has given every mother the *power.* He has placed in your hands a helpless babe, entirely dependent upon you; so that if it disobeys you, all you have to do is to cut off its sources of enjoyment, or inflict bodily pain, so steadily and so invariably that disobedience and suffering shall be indissolubly connected in the mind of the child. What more *power* can a parent ask for than God has already given? And if we fail to use this power for the purposes for which it was bestowed, the sin is ours, and upon us and upon our children must rest the consequences. The exercise of discipline must often be painful, but if you shrink from duty here, you expose yourself to all that sad train of woes which disobedient children leave behind them. If you cannot summon sufficient resolution to deprive of enjoyment and inflict pain when it is necessary, then you must feel that a broken heart and an old age of sorrow will not be unmerited. And when you look upon your dissolute sons and ungrateful daughters, you must remember that the time was when you might have checked their evil propensities. If you love momentary ease better than your children's welfare and your own permanent happiness, you cannot murmur at the lot you have freely chosen. And when you meet your children at the bar of God, and they point to you and say, "It was through your neglect of duty that we are banished from heaven, and consigned to endless woe," you must feel what no tongue can tell. Ah! It is dreadful for a mother to trifle with duty. Eternal destinies are committed to your trust. The influence you are now exerting will go on, unchecked by the grave or the judgment, and will extend onward through those ages to which there is no end.

CHAPTER THREE

Maternal Authority: Part II

Upon the subject of obedience there are a few other suggestions of importance to be made:

1 *First then, there is a very great diversity in the natural dispositions of children.* Some are very tender in their feelings, and easily governed by affection. Others are naturally independent and self-willed. Sometimes a child gets its passions excited and its will determined, and it cannot be subdued but by a very great effort. Almost every faithful mother is acquainted with such contests, and she knows that they often form a *crisis* in the character of the child. If the child then obtain the victory, it is almost impossible for the mother afterward to regain her authority. The child feels that he is the victor and his mother the vanquished; and it is with very great difficulty that he will be compelled to renounce his independence. If, on the other hand, the mother conquer, and the child is subdued, he feels that the question is settled, and he has but little disposition to resume hostilities with one who has proved herself superior. I have known many such contests, severe and protracted, which were exceedingly painful to a parent's feelings. But, when once entered upon, they must be continued till the child is subdued.

It is not safe, on *any account,* for the parent to give up and retire vanquished.

The following instance of such a contest occurred a few years ago. A gentleman, sitting by his fire side one evening, with his family around him, took the spelling-book and called upon one of his little sons to come and read: John was about four years old. He knew all the letters of the alphabet perfectly, but happened at that moment to be in rather a sullen humor, and was not at all disposed to gratify his father. Very reluctantly he came as he was bid, but when his father pointed with his knife to the first letter of the alphabet, and said, "What letter is that, John?" he could get no answer. John looked upon the book, sulky and silent.

"My son," said the father, pleasantly, "you know the letter A."

"I cannot say A," said John.

"You must," said the father, in a serious and decided tone. "What letter is that?"

John refused to answer. The contest was now fairly commenced. John was willful, and determined that he would not read. His father knew that it would be ruinous to his son to allow him to conquer. He felt that he must, at all hazards, subdue him. He took him into another room, and punished him. He then returned, and again showed John the letter. But John still refused to name it. The father again retired with his son, and punished him more severely. But it was unavailing; the stubborn child still refused to name the letter, and when told that it was *A,* declared that he could not say *A.* Again the father inflicted punishment as severely as he dared to do it, and still the child, with his whole frame in agitation, refused to yield.

The father was suffering from the most intense solicitude. He regretted exceedingly that he had been drawn into the contest. He had already punished his child with a severity which he feared to exceed. And yet the willful sufferer stood before him, sobbing and trembling, but apparently as unyielding as a rock. I have often heard that parent mention the acuteness of his feelings at that moment. His heart was bleeding at the pain which he had been compelled to inflict upon his son. He knew that the question was now to be settled, who should be master. And after his son had withstood so long and so much, he greatly feared the result. The mother sat by, suffering, of course, most acutely, but perfectly satisfied that it was their duty to subdue the child, and that in such a trying hour a mother's feelings must not interfere. With a heavy heart the father again took the hand of his son to lead him out of the room for farther punishment. But, to his inconceivable joy, the child shrunk from enduring any more suffering, and cried, "Father, I'll tell the letter." The father, with feelings not easily conceived, took the book and pointed to the letter.

"A," said John, distinctly and fully.

"And what is that?" said the father, pointing to the next letter.

"B," said John.

"And what is that?"

"C," he continued.

"And what is that?" pointing again to the first letter.

"A," said the now humbled child.

"Now carry the book to your mother, and tell her what the letter is."

"What letter is that, my son?" said the mother.

"A," said John. He was evidently perfectly subdued. The rest of the children were sitting by, and they saw the contest, and they saw where was the victory. And John learnt a lesson which he never forgot—that his father had an arm too strong for him. He learned never again to wage such an unequal warfare. He learnt that it was the safest and happiest course for him to obey.

But perhaps some one says it was cruel to punish the child so severely. Cruel! It was mercy and love. It would indeed have been cruel had the father, in that hour, been unfaithful, and shrunk from his painful duty. The passions he was then, with so much self-sacrifice, striving to subdue, if left unchecked, would, in all probability, have been a curse to their possessor, and have made him a curse to his friends. It is by no means improbable that upon the decisions of that hour depended the character and happiness of that child for life, and even for eternity. It is far from improbable that, had he then conquered, all future efforts to subdue him would have been in vain, and that he would have broken away from all restraint, and have been miserable in life, and lost in death. Cruelty! The Lord preserve children from the *tender mercies* of those who so regard such self-denying kindness.

It is always best, if possible, to avoid such collisions. Many children are taught implicit obedience without ever entering into such a contest with their parents. And it is certainly preferable to govern a child by the mild procedure of ordinary discipline, rather than enter into such a formidable conflict, where great severity is often required. Wisdom, therefore, teaches us to guard against giving a child an opportunity of summoning all its energies to disobey. They are peculiar occasions, and peculiar moods of mind, which generally elicit this strength of rebellious feeling. A little foresight will often enable us, without surrender of authority, to calm the rising feeling, instead of exciting it to its utmost strength. We may sometimes, by judicious management, check the rebellion in its first appearance, before it has gained sufficient strength to call all our power into exercise to put it down.

As an illustration, let us suppose that James and Mary are playing together in the evening, and James gets vexed and strikes his sister. He has done this without any provocation, and ought to be punished, and to ask his sister's forgiveness. But the mother has perceived that, during the whole day, James has manifested a very unpleasant disposition. He has been irritable and unyielding. She sees that now he is excited and angry. Every parent knows that such variations of feeling are not uncommon. One day a child is pleasant and affectionate; the next, every thing seems to go wrong; little things vex, and the whole disposition seems to be soured. The mother perceives that her son is in this frame of mind. He has done wrong, and ought to ask his sister's forgiveness. But she knows that, in this excited and unamiable frame of mind, he will be strongly tempted to resist her authority. Unreasonably vexed as he is, it would be one of the hardest acts of submission for him to ask the forgiveness of his sister. If the mother tells him to do so, the temptation to refuse is so strong, that, in all probability, he will decline obeying. She must then punish him. And here comes the contest, which must be continued, if it is commenced, till the child submits. Now, how is this contest to be avoided? By overlooking the fault? Most certainly not. The mother rises, takes James by the hand, and says, "My son, you have been doing very wrong; you are ill-humored, and must not stay with us any longer; I will carry you to bed." She accordingly leads him away to his chamber.

Just before leaving him for the night, she tells him in a kind but sorrowful tone, how much she is displeased, and how much God must be displeased with his conduct. As usual, she hears him say his prayers, or kneels by the bedside, and prays that God will forgive him. She then leaves him to his own reflections and to sleep.

He is thus punished for his fault. And as he lies in his bed, and hears his brothers and sisters happy down-stairs, he feels how much wiser and better it is to be a good boy. In the morning he awakes. Night has given repose to his excited feelings. He thinks how unhappy his yesterday's misconduct made him, and resolves to be more upon his guard for the future. All his rebellious feelings are quelled by the soothing influence of sleep. His passions are not aroused. The mother can now operate upon his mind without any fear of having a contest with a determined and stubborn will.

When the children come down in the morning, she calls James and Mary before her. Taking the hand of each, she mildly says, "My son, you made us all unhappy last night by striking your little sister; I hope you are sorry for what you did." "Yes, mother, I am" says James; being led easily now to the feelings of penitence and submission, to which, during the moments of irritation and excitement, he could not, at least without great difficulty, have been driven. Thus, by judicious management, the desired object is attained, and perfectly attained, while the contest is avoided. The fault is not overlooked, and James is humbled. But had the mother, regardless of the child's peculiar state of feeling, commanded him immediately to ask forgiveness of his sister, it would, in all probability, have led to a scene actually painful to both mother and son. And the final effect of the discipline would, perhaps, have been less beneficial upon the mind of the child. But cases will sometimes occur when it is not possible thus to wave the strife. When such an emergency rises, it is the duty of the parent boldly and resolutely to meet it. If, from false feeling, you then shrink, you are recreant[6] to the sacred trust which God has committed to your care. Is it kindness for a mother to let her child die, rather than compel it to take the bitter prescription which is to restore it to health and strength? And is it kindness to let those passions conquer, which, unsubdued, will be, for time and eternity, a scourge to their possessor? If there be any cruelty in the world which is truly dreadful, it is the cruelty of a falsely indulgent and unfaithful parent.

Let it be particularly understood, however, that all we here inculcate is firmness in the discharge of parental duty, in those cases where such collisions between parents and children are unavoidable. They can, however, in most cases, be avoided. If, for instance, a child disobeys you, you can simply punish it for the act of disobedience, and there let the difficulty end. It is not necessary that you should always require that the thing at first commanded should be done. You direct a little girl to give a book to her sister. She refuses; and you may take two distinct courses to maintain your violated authority. You may go and take the book yourself and give it to the sister, and then inflict

---

[6] Recreant – one who yields in combat and cries craven; hence, a mean-spirited, cowardly wretch.

such a punishment upon the disobedient one as the offence deserves. Or, you may insist upon obedience; and to enforce it, enter upon a contest which may be long and painful. Now, whichever of these plans you adopt, be firm and decided in the execution of it. The former is, however, in almost all cases, the wisest and best.

In the above remarks allusion has been made to the variations of feeling to which children are subject. No one, who has had any thing to do with education, can have failed to observe this. Almost every individual is conscious of seasons when he seems to be afflicted with a kind of morbid sensitiveness. Our spirits often rise and fall with bodily health; and he has gained a great victory over his body, and a great triumph of mind, who can invariably preserve the same calm and cheerful spirit, undisturbed by harassing cares, or the irritations of a diseased frame. The nervous system of some individuals is so delicately constructed, that an east wind, or a damp day, will completely unhinge the mind. When we see some of the wisest and best of men oppressed with these infirmities, we must learn forbearance and sympathy with children. At such times, a judicious mother, knowing that the irritability is as much a bodily as a mental infirmity, will do all in her power to calm and soothe. She will avoid every thing calculated to jar the feelings, and will endeavor, by mild amusements or repose, to lull these feelings asleep. By this method she will save the child much unhappiness, and will promote an amiable and sweet disposition. Probably many children have had their feelings permanently soured by utter disregard of these variations of mind. The disposition of a child is of too delicate a texture to be handled with a rough and careless grasp. Its affectionate and gentle feelings should be elicited by maternal sympathy and love. And we should endeavor to assuage its occasional irritability, by calling away the mind from objects of unpleasant excitement, and alluring it to cheering contemplations.

It is clear that there is a striking difference in the natural dispositions of children; but nothing can be more evident than that a good disposition may be soured by mismanagement, and that a child of naturally unamiable feelings may, by judicious culture become mild and lovely. The cultivation of the disposition is an important part of education. Hence the necessity of studying the moods and the feelings of the child, and of varying the discipline to meet these changes. Cases will undoubtedly arise, when the parent will find it difficult to judge what is duty. Such cases will, however, be infrequent. The obvious general policy is, when a child is in this excited state, to remove him as much as possible from the power of temptation. And if he commits a fault which it is necessary to notice, let the punishment be of such a kind as is calculated to soothe him. For instance, give him a comfortable seat by the fire, and tell him that he must not leave the chair for half an hour. Place in his hand some pleasing book, or some plaything which will amuse him. In this way let the punishment be adapted to the peculiarity of the moral disorder.

This is not the mockery of punishment which it may seem. The child feels it to be real, and it is of a nature to operate beneficially. Some faults, however, he may commit, which, under the circumstances of the case, it may be inexpedient to notice. He may speak peevishly to his sister. The mother does not *appear* to notice it; she, however, sees the importance of immediately allaying this peevish spirit, and she endeavors to plan some amusement which will promote good humor. Perhaps she lays down her work and joins the children in their amusements, till, through her happy influence, cheerfulness and good humor are restored.

"Here, my son," perhaps she says, "I should like to have you take your slate, and sit down in your chair, and see if you can draw some animal so correctly that I can tell what it is. And Maria, you may take your slate and chair, and sit by his side, and do the same."

The children are quite animated with their new play. They are soon busily at work, and whispering together, that their mother may not hear what animals they are drawing. By this simple artifice, the little cloud of irritated feeling which was rising is entirely dispelled. Had the mother, on the other hand, punished the child for the incidental peevishness of remark, the mind would not have been so speedily or so pleasantly brought into its desired state. Or, had the mother taken no notice of the occurrence, the disposition of the child would have been injured by the allowed increase of the ill-humor, and, in all probability, a quarrel might soon have ensued. Constant watchfulness, on the part of the mother, will soon enable her to foresee many dangers, and prevent many difficulties.

2. Never punish when the child has not intentionally done wrong. Children are often very unjustly punished. Things which are really wrong are overlooked, and again, punishment is inflicted on account of some accident, when the child is entirely innocent. Such a course of procedure not only destroys, in the mind of the child, the distinction between accident and crime, but is in itself absolutely iniquitous. The parent has all the power, and she may be the most relentless tyrant, and the child

These illustrations are sufficient to show the importance of making allowance for ignorance, and for accidents. And they also show how frequently children suffer, when they are not to blame. If a child s punished when innocent, as well as when guilty, the distinction between right and wrong is obliterated from his mind. Hence it becomes an important rule in family government, never to punish when the child has not intentionally done wrong.

3. Never think that your child is too young to obey. We are ingenious in framing excuses for neglecting our duty with our children. At one time they are too young; again they are too sick. Some parents always find an excuse, of one kind or another, for letting their children have their own way. A child may, at a very early age, be taught obedience. We can easily teach a kitten, or a little dog, that it must not touch the meat which is placed before the fire, that it must leave the room when bidden, and a thousand other acts of ready obedience.

A Frenchman has recently collected a large number of canary birds for a show. He has taught them such implicit obedience to his voice, as to march them in platoons across the room, and directs them to the ready performance of many simple maneuvers. Now, can it be admitted that a child, fifteen months or two years of age, is inferior in understanding to a canary bird? And must the excuse be made for such a child, that he does not know enough to be taught obedience? A very judicious mother, who has brought up a large family of children, all of whom are now in situations of respectability and usefulness, remarked that it was her practice to obey her children for the first year of their life, but ever after she expected them to obey her. She, of course, did not mean by this remark, that the moment the child was one year of age a sudden and total change took place in her management. During the early months of its infancy she considered it to be her duty to do every thing in her power to make the child comfortable and happy. She would endeavor to anticipate all its wants. She would be obedient to the wishes of the child. But, by the time the child was one year of age, she considered it old enough to be brought under the salutary regulations of a well disciplined family.

I am aware that many parents will say that this is altogether too early a period to commence the government of a child, and others equally numerous, perhaps, will say that it is too late; that a beginning should be made at a much earlier period. In fact, the principle which really ought to guide in such a case, is this: that the authority of the mother ought to be established over the child as soon as it is able to understand a command or prohibition expressed by looks and gestures. This is at a much earlier period than most parents imagine. Let the mother who doubts it try the experiment, and see how easily she can teach her child that he must not touch the tongs or andirons; or that, when sitting in her lap at table, he must not touch the cups and saucers. A child may be taught obedience in such things then, as well as at any period of its life. And how much trouble does a mother save herself, by having her child thus early taught to obey! How much pain and sorrow does she save her child by accustoming it, in its most tender years, to habits of prompt obedience.

4. *Guard against too much severity.* By pursuing a steady course of efficient government, severity will very seldom be found necessary. If, when punishment is inflicted, it is done

with composure and with solemnity; occasions for punishment will be very infrequent. Let a mother ever be affectionate and mild with her children. Let her sympathize with them in their little sports. Let her gain their confidence by her assiduous efforts to make them happy. And let her feel, when they have done wrong, not irritated, but sad; and punish them in sorrow, but not in anger. Fear is a useful and a necessary principle in family government. God makes use of it in governing his creatures. But it is ruinous to the disposition of a child, exclusively to control him by this motive. How unhappy must be that family where the parent always sits with a face deformed with scowls, and where the voice is always uttered in tones of severity and command! Such parents we do see. Their children fear them. They are always under restraint in their presence; and home becomes to them an irksome prison, instead of the happy retreat of peace and joy. But where the mother greets her children with smiles; and rewards their efforts to please her, with caresses; and addresses them in tones of mildness and affection, she is touching those chords in the human heart which vibrate in sweet harmony; she is calling into action the noblest and the loveliest principles of our nature. And thus does she prepare the way for every painful act of discipline to come with effectual power upon the heart. The children know that she does not love to punish. In all cases in which it can be done, children should thus be governed by kindness. But when kindness fails, and disobedience ensues, let not the mother hesitate for a moment to fall back upon her last resort, and punish as severely as is necessary. A few such cases will teach almost any child how much better it is to be obedient than disobedient.

By being thus consistent and decided in government, and commencing with the infancy of each child, in all ordinary cases great severity may be avoided. And it is never proper for a parent to be harsh, and unfeeling, and forbidding, in her intercourse with her children. The most efficient family government may be almost entirely administered by affection, if it be distinctly understood that disobedience cannot pass unpunished. I cannot but pity those unhappy children who dare not come to their parents in confidence and love; who are continually fearing stern looks and harsh words; and who are consequently ever desirous to get away from home, that they may enjoy themselves. Every effort should be made to make home the most desirable place; to gather around it associations of delight; and thus to form in the mind of your child an attachment for peaceful and purifying enjoyments. This will most strongly fortify his mind against vice. And when he leaves the paternal roof, he will ever look back with fond recollections to its joys, and with gratitude to those who made it the abode of so much happiness. In future years, too, when your children become the heads of families, they will transmit to their children the principles which you have implanted. Thus may the influence of your instructions extend to thousands yet unborn.

How little do we think of the tremendous responsibilities which are resting upon us; and of the wide influence, either for good or for evil, which we are exerting! We are setting in operation a train of causes which will go down through all coming time. Long after we have gone to our eternal home, our words and our actions will be aiding in the formation of character. We cannot then arrest the causes which our lives have set in progress, and they will go on elevating immortals to virtue and to heaven or urging them onward in passion and sin, and woe.

CHAPTER FOUR

The Mother's Difficulties

The remarks which have already been made are so obvious, that one is led to inquire, why is family government generally so defective? Why do so few succeed in obtaining prompt obedience? There are many causes operating to produce this result. The rules of discipline may be simple and plain, and yet many motives may influence us to shrink from enforcing them.

1. *One great obstacle is the want of self-control on the part of parents.* How few persons are there who have gained that conquest over self, which enables them to meet the various vicissitudes of life with calmness and composure! How few are there who are not, occasionally at least, thrown off their guard, and provoked to the exhibition of excited and irritated feeling! And can a mother expect to govern her child when she cannot govern herself? Family government must most emphatically begin at *home*. It must begin in the bosom of the parent. She must learn to control herself; to subdue her own passions; she must set her children an example of meekness and of equanimity, or she must reasonably expect that all her efforts to control their passions will be ineffectual. A child gets irritated

and strikes his sister; and the mother gets irritated and whips the child. Now, both mother and child have been guilty of precisely the same crime. They have both been angry, and both in anger have struck another. And what is the effect of this sinful punishment? It may make the child afraid to strike his sister again; but will it teach that child that he has done wrong; that it is wicked to be angry? Can it have any salutary effect upon his heart? He sees that his mother is irritated, and thus is he taught that it is proper for him to be angry. He sees that when his mother is irritated *she strikes;* and thus is he taught that the same course is proper for him. The direct effect of the punishment is to feed the flame and strengthen the inveteracy[7] of passion. In such a course as this there is no moral instruction, and no salutary discipline. And yet a mother who has not conquered self, who cannot restrain the violence of her own passions, will often thus punish. When we see such a mother with passionate and turbulent children, no second question need be asked why they are not gentle and obedient. And when we reflect how very seldom it is that we see an individual who may not be occasionally provoked to act from the irritation of the moment, we cannot wonder that the family so often presents a scene of uproar and misrule.

This self-control, at all times, and under all circumstances, is one of the most important and most difficult things to be acquired. Many parents have, from infancy, been unaccustomed to restraint, and they find a very great struggle to be necessary to smother those feelings which will sometimes rise almost involuntarily. But we should ever remember that this must be

---

[7] Inveteracy – long continuance, or firmness or deep-rooted obstinacy of any quality or state acquired by time.

done, or we cannot be faithful to our children. We must bring our own feelings and our own actions under a system of rigid discipline, or it will be in vain for us to hope to curb the passions and restrain the conduct of those who are looking to us for instruction and example. There will many cases occur which will exceedingly try a mother's patience. Unless naturally blest with a peculiarly quiet spirit, or habituated from early life to habits of self-government, she will find that she has very much to do with her own heart. This point we would most earnestly urge, for it is of fundamental importance. Anger is temporary insanity. And what can be more deplorable than to see a mother in the paroxysm of irritation, taking vengeance on her child? Let a mother feel grieved, and manifest her grief when her child does wrong. Let her, with calmness and reflection; use the discipline which the case requires. But never let her manifest irritated feeling, or give utterance to an angry expression. If her own mind is thus kept serene and unimpassioned, she will instruct by example as well as precept. She will easily know, and more judiciously perform her duty. And the superiority of her own conduct will command the respect and the admiration of her children. And until this is done, it will be impossible for a mother to enforce the rules of discipline, simple and obvious as those rules are.

 2. Another great obstacle in the way is the lack of resolution. It is always painful to a parent's feelings to deprive a child of any reasonable enjoyment, or to inflict pain. Hence we are ingenious in framing apologies to relieve ourselves from this duty. Your child does wrong, and you know that he ought to be punished; but you shrink from the duty of inflicting it. Now, of what avail is it to be acquainted with the rules of discipline, if we cannot summon resolution to enforce those rules? It will do no good to read one book and another upon the subject of education, unless we are willing, with calm and steady decision, to punish our children when the occasion requires. It is this weak indulgence, this wicked refusal to perform painful duty, which has ruined thousands of families. A mother will sometimes openly remonstrate with a father for punishing a stubborn child. She will call him cruel and unfeeling, and confirm her child in his willfulness, by her wicked sympathy and caresses.

What can be expected from such a course as this? Such a mother is the most cruel and merciless enemy which her child can have. Under such an influence he will probably grow up in wretchedness, not only to curse the day in which he was born, but to heap still bitterer curses upon the mother who bore him. You can do nothing more ruinous to your child; you can do nothing which will more effectually teach him to hate and despise you; you can do nothing which will, with more certainty, bring you in sorrow and disgrace to the grave, than thus to allow maternal feelings to influence you to neglect painful but necessary acts of discipline.

I would ask the mother who reads this book, if she has not often been conscious of a struggle between the sense of duty and inclination. Duty has told you to punish your child. Inclination has urged you to overlook its disobedience. Inclination has triumphed; and your child has retired victorious, and of course confirmed in his sin. Be assured that thus, in your own heart, lies one of the greatest obstacles to your success; and until this obstacle be surmounted, every thing else will be unavailing. It would by no means be difficult to fill this volume with cases illustrative of this fact, and of the awful consequences resulting.

A few years ago, a lady was left a widow, with several little sons. She loved them most devotedly. The affliction which she had experienced in the loss of her husband, fixed her affections with more intensity of ardor and sensitiveness upon her children. They were her only hope. Sad and joyless as she was, she could not endure to punish them, or to deprive them of a single indulgence. Unhappy and misguided woman! Could she expect to escape the consequences of such a course? She was living upon the delusive hope that her indulgences would ensure their love. And now one of these sons is seventeen years of age, a stout, and turbulent and self-willed boy. He is altogether beyond the influence of maternal restraint. He is the tyrant of the family, and his afflicted mother is almost entirely brokenhearted by this accumulation of sorrow. The rest of the children are coming on in the same path. She sees and trembles in view of the calamity, which it is now too late to avert. It would be far happier for her to be childless, as well as a widow. Her children are her oppressors. She is their slave. It is impossible now to retrace her steps, or to retrieve the injury she has done her children and herself. Hardly any situation can be conceived more truly pitiable. And what has caused this magnitude of sorrow? Simply the mother's reluctance to do her duty. She looked upon her poor fatherless children with all the tender emotions of a widowed mother, and could not bear to throw around them necessary restraint, and insist upon obedience to her commands. She knew perfectly well, that when they were disobedient, they ought to be punished; that it was her duty to enforce her authority. It was not her ignorance which caused this dreadful wreck of happiness; it was the want of resolution—that fond, and foolish, and cruel tenderness, which induced her to consult her own feelings rather than the permanent welfare of her children.

The reader will, perhaps, inquire whether this statement is a true account of a real case. It is a true account of a thousand cases all over our land. Mothers, we appeal to your observation, if you do not see, every where around you, these wrecks of earthly hopes. Have we not warnings enough to avoid this fatal rock? and yet it is the testimony of all who have moved about the world with an observing eye, that this parental irresolution is one of the most prominent causes of domestic afflictions.

There must be energy of character, or acts of discipline will be so inefficient as to do more harm than good. The spirit will be irritated, but not subdued. Punishment becomes a petty vexation, and its influence is most decidedly pernicious. It is of the utmost importance, that when it is inflicted, it should be serious and effectual. And it is certain that the mother who adopts prompt and decisive measures, will go forward with far less trouble to herself and her child, and will, on the whole, inflict far less pain than the one who adopts the feeble and dilatory measures which we so often see. While the one must be continually threatening, and inflicting that mockery of punishment which is just enough to irritate the temper and spoil the disposition; the other will usually find her word promptly obeyed, and will very seldom find it necessary to punish at all.

But few persons have obtained a more correct knowledge of human nature than Bonaparte; and but few have ever acquired such a control over the human mind. It is said that there was once a formidable mob rioting in the streets of Paris, and carrying devastation wherever they went. One of his generals was sent out with a body of infantry to disperse the mob. He read the riot act. They laughed at it. He threatened to fire upon them. They defied him. He opened upon them a fire with blank cartridges. As volley after volley was discharged, and not a man fell, the mob laughed to scorn their impotent efforts. At last the general was compelled to load with real bullets. But by this time the passions of the mob were so excited, and they had become so familiar with the harmless discharge of musketry, that they stood firm when the bullets came. They were gradually prepared for it. A pitched battle was the result; and it was not till after an immense massacre that the infuriated populace was dispersed.

At another time, when the ravages of a Parisian mob were scattering terror through the city, Bonaparte led on, at a quick step, several companies of artillery. Immediately upon arriving at the scene of devastation, the soldiers, retiring to the right and left, opened upon the riotous multitude the formidable cannon. Not a word was said; not a moment of hesitation intervened; but at once the voice of Bonaparte was heard in the thunders of the artillery, and the compact mass of the multitude was ploughed through by the cannon ball. The mob, unprepared for such decisive measures, and terrified at the havoc, fled with the utmost precipitancy in every direction. Then did he pour in his blank cartridges. Peal after peal thundered through the streets, adding to the consternation of the affrighted multitude, and in less than five minutes scarce a solitary straggler was to be seen. Such were the measures which this extraordinary man adopted, and which gave him an ascendancy over the public mind almost unparalleled in the history of man. Some one afterward suggested to him that it might have been more merciful, if he had first tried the effect of blank charges, and then, if necessary, had proceeded to extremities. But he very justly replied that by such tardy measures the mob would have had time to collect their courage, and many more would have fallen before they would have fled. The principle illustrated in this anecdote is of universal application. Real benevolence prompts to decisive measures. The mother who first coaxes; then threatens; then pretends to punish; then punishes a little; is only making trouble for herself and sorrow for her family. But, on the other hand, if she promptly meets acts of disobedience, and with firmness, and inflicts necessary punishment decidedly, and at once, she is, in the most effectual way, promoting her own happiness, and the best welfare of her child.

A parent is much more prone to be thus fatally indulgent, if a child is of a feeble and sickly constitution. Such children are very generally spoiled. How strange, when God, in his mysterious providence, lays his hand upon some little one, and causes it to languish in weakness and in suffering, that the parent on that very account should neglect that child's welfare, and allow its passions to grow unchecked, its will to be stubborn and unsubdued! The mother perhaps is willing to do her duty with her more robust son. She will do all in her power to control his passions, and make him a good and happy boy. But the poor little sufferer she will indulge in all its caprices, till passion is strong and irritability is unconquerable, and the deeper sorrows of the mind are thus added to the pains and weakness of the body. O how much cruelty there is in the world which goes by the false name of tenderness or love!

Mother, have you a sick and suffering child? You are to that child a guardian angel, if with mild and affectionate decision you enforce your authority. Punish that child if it be necessary to teach him habitually and promptly to obey. If you do not do this, you are the bitterest enemy your child can have. You are doing that which has the most direct tendency to perpetuate its feebleness and to promote its misery. And yet I know that some mothers will still say, "What, speak authoritatively, and even punish a poor little child when sick! How unfeeling!" There, there is the difficulty. Unkind to do all in your power to make your child patient and happy! A little girl we will suppose cuts deeply her hand. Her mother is *so kind* that she will not let a physician be called, for fear he should hurt her daughter in probing and dressing the wound. Day after day this *kind mother* beholds the increasing and extending inflammation. She strives in her ignorance to assuage the agony of the wound, till, after many days of excruciating suffering, the physician is called to save her daughter's life by amputating the limb. When the accident first occurred, a few moments of attention and trifling pain would have prevented all these dreadful consequences.

But the conduct of that mother is far more cruel, who will allow the *mind's inflammation* to increase and extend unchecked; who, rather than inflict the momentary pain which is necessary to subdue the stubborn will, and allay irritation, will allow the moral disorder to gain such strength as to be incurable. The consequences thus resulting are far more disastrous. They affect man's immortal nature, and go on through eternity. There is no cruelty so destructive as this.

Yet let it not be supposed that austerity is recommended. This is unnecessary, and is always to be avoided. Let the tones of the voice be affectionate and soothing. Let the mother sympathize with her whole heart in the trials and sufferings of her child. Let her be ingenious in devices for its amusement. But let her not ruin her precious treasure by indulging it in peevishness or disobedience. Your child cannot possibly be happy, unless taught to subdue his passions and to be obedient to your will. We would have kindness, and gentleness, and love, ever diffusing joy through the family circle. But if you would see your children happy, and be happy yourself, you must, when your children are in sickness, as well as when they are in health, summon sufficient resolution to ensure propriety of behavior and obedience to your commands.

Be firm then in doing your duty invariably. Never refrain from governing your child because it is painful to maternal feelings. It is certainly wisely ordered by Providence that it should be painful to a parent's heart to inflict suffering upon a child. He who can punish without sympathy, without emotions of sorrow, cannot punish with a right spirit. Even our Father ill heaven does not willingly afflict his children. But does he on that account withhold his discipline, and allow us to go on in sin unpunished? We must, in earnest prayer, look to him for strength and wisdom, and religiously do our duty. We must be willing to have our own hearts bleed, if we can thus save our children from the ravages of those passions which, unchecked, will ruin their usefulness and peace.

A child, a short time ago, was taken sick with that dangerous disorder, the croup. It was a child most ardently beloved, and ordinarily very obedient. But in this state of uneasiness and pain he refused to take the medicine which it was needful without delay to administer. The father, finding him resolute, immediately punished his sick and suffering son. Under these circumstances, and fearing that his son might soon die, it must have been a most severe trial to the father. But the consequence was that the child was taught that sickness was no excuse for disobedience. And while his sickness continued, he promptly took whatever medicine was prescribed, and was patient and submissive. Soon the child was well. Does any one say this was cruel? It was one of the noblest acts of kindness which could have been performed. If the father had shrunk from duty here, it is by no means improbable that the life of the child would have been the forfeit. And this is the way to acquire strength of resolution, by *practicing* strength of resolution in every case. We must readily and promptly do our duty, be it ever so painful.

3. Another great obstacle in the way of training up a happy and virtuous family, is the occasional lack of harmony between parents on the subject of education. Sometimes, when a father is anxious to do his duty, the mother is a weak and foolish woman, who thinks that every punishment, and every deprivation of indulgence, is cruelty to her children. And when any one of them is punished, she will, by her caresses, do away the effect of the discipline, and convey to the mind of the child the impression that his father is cruel and unjust. A man who has formed so unhappy a union is indeed in a deplorable condition. And if his wife is incapable of being convinced of the ruinous consequences of such a course, he must take upon himself the whole duty of government. But as I am not now writing to fathers, I must turn from this case to another.

It not infrequently happens that a judicious and faithful mother is united with a husband whose principles and example are any thing but what she could desire. In such cases, not only does the whole government of the family devolve upon the mother but the influence of the father is such as, in a great degree, to counteract all her exertions. This is indeed a trying situation. It is, however, far from being a hopeless one. You must not give up in despair, but let the emergencies of the case rouse you to more constant watchfulness, and more persevering and vigorous effort. If a wife be judicious and consistent in her exertions, a father, in almost all cases, will soon feel confidence in her management of her family, and will very gladly allow her to bear all the burden of taking care of the children. Such a father is almost necessarily, much of the time, absent from home, and when at home, is not often in a mood to enjoy the society of his family. Let such a mother teach her children to be quiet and still when their father is present. Let her make every effort to accustom them to habits of industry. And let her do every thing in her power to induce them to be respectful, and obedient, and affectionate to their father. This course is indeed the best which can be adopted to reclaim the unhappy parent. The more cheerful you can make home to him, the stronger are the inducements which are presented to draw him away from scenes into which he ought not to enter.

It is true there is no situation more difficult than the one we are now describing. But, that even these difficulties are not insurmountable, facts have not infrequently proved. Many cases occur, in which the mother triumphantly surmounts them all, and rears up a virtuous and happy family. Her husband is most brutally intemperate; and I need not here depict the scenes through which such a mother is called to pass. She sees, however, that the welfare of the family is dependent upon her, and accordingly nerves her heart, resolutely, to meet her responsibilities. She commences, in the earliest infancy of her children, teaching them implicit obedience. She binds them to her with those ties from which they never would be able or desirous to break. The most abundant success rewards her efforts. The older her children grow the more respectful and attentive they become, for the more clearly they see that they are indebted to their mother for salvation from their father's disgrace and woe. Every sorrow of such a mother is alleviated by the sympathy and affection of her sons. She looks around upon them with feelings of maternal gratification, which no language can describe. They feel the worth and the dignity of her character. Though her situation in life may be humble, and though her mind may not be stored with knowledge, her moral worth, and her judicious government, command their reverence.

In a family of this sort, in a neighboring state, one cold December night, the mother was sitting alone by the fire, between the hours of nine and ten, waiting for the return of her absent husband. Her sons, fatigued with the labors of the day, had all retired to rest. A little before ten, her husband came in from the neighboring store, where he had passed the evening with his degraded associates. He insisted upon calling up the boys at that unseasonable hour, to send into the wood lot for a load of wood. Though there was an ample supply of fuel at the house, he would not listen to reason, but stamped and swore that the boys should go. The mother, finding it utterly in vain to oppose his wishes, called her sons, and told them that their father insisted upon their going with the team to the wood lot. She spoke to them kindly; told them she was sorry they must go; but, said she, "Remember that he is your father." Her sons were full grown young men. But at their mother's voice they immediately rose, and, without a murmur, brought out the oxen, and went to the woods. They had perfect confidence in her judgment and her management. While they were absent, their mother was busy in preparing an inviting supper for them upon their return. The drunken father soon retired. About midnight the sons finished their task, and entering the house, found their mother ready to receive them with cheerfulness and smiles. A bright fire was blazing on the hearth. The room was warm and pleasant. With keen appetites and that cheerfulness of spirits which generally accompanies the performance of duty, those children sat down with their much-loved parent to the repast she had provided, and soon after all were reposing in the quietude and the silence of sleep.

Many a mother has thus been the guardian and the savior of her family. She has brought up her sons to industry, and her daughters to virtue. And in her old age she has reaped a rich reward for all her toil, in the affections and the attentions of her grateful children. She has struggled, in tears and discouragement, for many weary years, till at last God has dispelled all the gloom, and filled her heart with joy in witnessing the blessed results of her fidelity. Be not, therefore, desponding. That which has once been done may be done again.

From what has been said in this chapter, it appears that self-control and resolution are the two all-important requisites in family government. With these two qualifications, which a person is inexcusable in not possessing, almost every other obstacle may be surmounted. Without these, your toil and solicitude will, in all probability, be in vain.

Your faithful exertions, attended with God's ordinary blessing, will open to you daily new sources of enjoyment in the unfolding virtues and expanding faculties of your children. Your decisive government will, most undoubtedly, be rewarded with the affection and respect of those whom you are training up to usefulness and happiness. And when old age comes, your children will welcome you to their homes, and rejoice to give you a seat by their fire-side, and by unabated attentions will do all in their power to prove how deeply they feel that debt of gratitude which never can be fully repaid. Such joys will obliterate the remembrance of all present toils and sorrows. Let these hopes cheer you to go on rejoicing in the path of duty.

CHAPTER FIVE

Faults and Errors

There are many faults in family government, which have been handed down from generation to generation, and have become almost universally diffused. They are so general, and we have been so long accustomed to them, that their glaring impropriety escapes our notice. The increasing interest now felt in the subject of education, by leading parents to read and to think, has taught many to avoid those errors which still very generally prevail. There are many parents who have not facilities for obtaining books upon this subject, and who have not been led to reflect very deeply upon their responsibilities. Some of these errors are such, that an apology seems almost necessary for cautioning mothers against them, since common sense so plainly condemns them. But let it be remembered, how large a portion of the mothers of our land are, by their situation, deprived of those sources of information and excitements to thought, which God has conferred upon others.

1. *Do not talk about children in their presence.* We are very apt to think that children do not understand what we say to one another, because they are unable to join in the conversation

themselves. But a child's comprehension of language is far in advance of his ability to use it. I have been much surprised at the result of experiments upon this subject. A little child creeping upon the floor, and who could not articulate a single word, was requested to carry a piece of paper across the room and put it in a chair. The child perfectly comprehended the direction, and crept across the room, and did as he was bidden. An experiment or two of this kind will satisfy any one how far a child's mind is in advance of his power to express his ideas. And yet, when a child is three or four years old, parents will relate in their presence shrewd things which they have said and done; sometimes even their acts of disobedience will be mentioned with a smile. The following conversation once passed between a lady and a mother, whose child, three years of age, was standing by her side.

"How does little Charles do?" said the lady.

"O," replied the mother, with a smile, "he is pretty well, but he is the greatest rogue you ever saw; I can do nothing with him."

"Why?" said the lady; "he does not look like a stubborn child."

"No," the mother replied, "he has not a bad disposition, but," she continued, smiling, "he is so *fond* of mischief that I can never make him mind me. He knows that he must not touch the andirons, but just before you came in he went and put one of his fingers on the brass, and looked me directly in the face. I told him he must take off his hand; and he put another finger on. I tried to look cross at him; but he, instead of stopping, rubbed his whole hand over the brass, and then ran away, laughing as heartily as he could. He did it, I suppose, on purpose to plague me, he is such a rogue."

Chapter Five – Faults and Errors

We insert this rather undignified story that the mothers who may read this chapter may know exactly what we mean by the caution we are urging. Now, to say nothing of that maternal unfaithfulness which would permit such acts of disobedience, how ruinous upon the mind of the child must be the effect of hearing his conduct thus spoken of and applauded! This perverse little fellow was more interested in the narration than either mother or visitor, and the impression produced upon his mind was stronger. The child was taught a lesson of disobedience, not soon to be forgotten.

There are many little artifices which a child will practice, which are decidedly to be discountenanced, but at which a parent can scarce refrain from smiling. These proofs of mental quickness and ingenuity are gratifying to parental feelings. They give promise of a mind susceptible of a high degree of cultivation, if properly guided and restrained. And there, are playful and affectionate feats of childhood which are pleasing on every account. They show good feelings, as well as an active intellect. Parents will speak to one another of those innumerable little occurrences which are daily gratifying them. But if these things are mentioned in the presence of the child, and applauded, its little heart is puffed up with vanity. How slight a degree of flattery will often awaken emotions of the most disgusting self-conceit, even in individuals of mature minds! How few persons are there who can bear praise! Vanity is almost a universal sin. None are so low, and none are so high, as to be freed from its power. And can *a child* bear, uninjured, that praise which has ruined so many *men?* Here lies one cause of the self-conceit so often visible in the nursery. We flatter our children without being conscious that they are so greedily drinking in the flattery. We do not give them credit for the amount of understanding they actually possess. It is true, almost all children are regarded by their parents as usually intelligent. This arises from the fact, that we are daily observing the unfoldings of the minds of the little ones who surround our firesides, while we have no opportunity of noticing the mental developements of others. But notwithstanding all this strength of parental partiality, we ordinarily consider children far less intelligent than they in reality are; and a mother will often talk as unguardedly in the presence of her child, who is three or four years of age, as she did in the presence of her infant of so many months. The necessity of caution upon this subject will be obvious to every parent upon a moment's reflection. Let nothing be said in the hearing of a child that would tend to excite its vanity. Guard against the possibility of his supposing that he does and says remarkable things, and is superior to other children.

But though a parent may restrain her own tongue, it is more difficult to restrain the tongues of others. Many visitors make it a constant habit to flatter the children wherever they go. Regardless of the ruinous effects upon their tender and susceptible minds, they think only of pleasing the parents. Beautiful children are thus peculiarly exposed. How common is it for a child of handsome countenance to have a spoiled temper! This is so frequently the case, that many persons have supposed that "spoiled beauty" are words never to be separated. I once knew a little boy, of unusually bright and animated countenance. Every one who entered the house, noticed the child, and spoke of his beauty. One day a gentleman called upon business, and being engaged in conversation, did not pay that attention to the child to which he was accustomed, and which he now began to expect as his due. The vain little fellow made many efforts to attract notice, but not succeeding, he at last placed himself full in front of the gentleman, and asked, "Why don't you see how beautiful I be?" The feeling, it is true, is not often so openly expressed, but nothing is more common than for it to be excited in precisely this way.

It is surely a duty to approve children when they do right, and to disapprove when they do wrong. But great caution should be used to preserve a child from hearing any thing which will destroy that most lovely trait of character—an humble spirit. It is, on this account, often a misfortune to a child to be unusually handsome or forward. It is so difficult to preserve it from the contaminations of flattery, that what might have been a great benefit becomes a serious injury.

2. Do not make exhibitions of your children's attainments. And here we must refer again to the danger of exciting vanity. There is no passion more universal, or with greater difficulty subdued. An eminent clergyman was once leaving his pulpit, when one of his parishioners addressed him, highly commending the sermon he had just uttered. "Be careful, my friend," said the clergyman, "I carry a tinderbox in my bosom." And if the bosom of an aged man of piety and of prayer may be thus easily inflamed, must there not be great danger in *showing off* a child to visitors, who will most certainly flatter its performance? You have taught your daughter some interesting hymns. She is modest and unassuming, and repeats them with much propriety. A friend calls, and you request the child to repeat her hymns. She does it. Thus far there is, perhaps, no injury done. But as soon as she has finished, your friend begins to flatter. Soon another and another friend calls, and the scene is continually repeated, till your daughter feels proud of her performance. She becomes indeed quite an actress. And the hymn which was intended to lead her youthful heart to God does but fill that heart with pride. Must it not be so? How can a child withstand such strong temptations? Parents may show their children that they are gratified in witnessing their intellectual attainments. And this presents a motive sufficiently strong to stimulate them to action. But when they are exposed to the indiscriminate and injudicious flattery of whoever may call, it is not for a moment to be supposed that they will retain just views of themselves. It must however be allowed, that, with some children, the danger is much greater than with others. Some need much encouragement, while others need continual restraint. Who has not noticed the thousand arts which a vain child will practice, simply to attract attention? Who has not seen such a spoiled one take a book and read, occasionally casting a furtive[8] glance from the page to the visitor, to see if the studious habit is observed? And can such a child be safely *exhibited* to strangers? It may, perhaps, at times, be an advantage to a modest child to repeat a hymn, or something of that nature, to a judicious friend. If your pastor feels that interest in children which he ought to cherish, he will regard all the little ones of his congregation with parental affection. He ought not to be considered as a stranger in the family. Children may appear before him with confidence and affection, and if he has the spirit of his Master, he will cautiously guard against flattery, and endeavor to improve the occasion by leading the mind to serious thoughts. But the practice of making a show of

---

[8] Furtive – stolen; obtained by theft; hence a picture of pride.

children, of exhibiting their little attainments, is certainly reprehensible; and it is, we fear, not only common, but increasing. The following remarks upon this subject are from the pen of an individual who combines much shrewdness of observation with extensive experience.

"I always felt pain for poor little things set up before company to repeat verses, or bits of plays, at six or eight years old. I have sometimes not known which way to look, when a mother, (and, too often a father,) whom I could not but respect on account of her fondness for her child, has forced the feeble-voiced eighth wonder of the world to stand with its little hand stretched out, shouting the soliloquy of Hamlet, or some such thing. I do not know any thing much more distressing to the spectators than exhibitions of this sort. Upon these occasions no one knows what to say, or whither to direct his looks. If I had to declare, on my oath, which have been the most disagreeable moments of my life, I verily believe that, after due consideration, I should fix upon those in which parents whom I have respected, have made me endure exhibitions like these; for this is your choice, to be insincere, or to give offence. The plaudits which the child receives in such cases puff it up in its own thoughts, and send it out into the world stuffed with pride and insolence, which must and will be extracted from it by one means or another. Now parents have *no right* thus to indulge their own feelings at the risk of the happiness of their children."

Scenes similar to those above described will at once occur to the recollection of the reader. And the fact that such are the feelings of many strangers, in general, is of itself amply sufficient to discountenance the practice.

There are two extremes which it is necessary to avoid. The one is that of secluding children altogether from society; the other is, of wearying our friends by their presence and their ceaseless talk. If we consider our children as troubles, to be kept out of the way whenever we wish for social enjoyment; if the entrance of a few friends to pass the evening is the signal for their immediate departure to another room, how can we expect them to improve, or to become acquainted with the proprieties of life? They must listen to the conversation and observe the manners of their superiors, that their minds and their manners may be improved. Not long ago I heard a gentleman speaking of an unusually interesting family he had just visited. It was known that he was coming to pass the evening. As he entered the room he saw three little children sitting quietly and silently by the fire. The mother was sitting by the table with her sewing. The father was rising to receive him. The children remained for an hour or more, listening with interest to the conversation which passed between their parents and the gentleman. They made not the least interruption, but by their presence and cheerful looks contributed much to the enjoyment of the evening. At eight o'clock the mother said, "Children, it is eight." Without another word, they all rose and left the room. The mother soon followed, and after being absent a few moments, returned. Now how much enjoyment is there in such a family as this! And how much improvement do the children derive from being accustomed to the society of their superiors! In this way they are taught humility, for they see how much less they know than others. They gain information, and their minds are strengthened by the conversation they hear. Their manners are improved, for children learn more by example than precept. If you would enjoy these pleasures, and confer upon your children these benefits, it is indispensable that they be habitually well governed. Nothing can be more hopeless than to expect that children will conduct properly when company is present, if at other times they are uncontrolled.

Some parents, feeling the importance that their children should enjoy good society, and at the same time having them under no restraint, deprive themselves and their visitors of all enjoyment, and their children of all benefit. We do not like, even in imagination, to encounter the deafening clamor of such a scene. Some are lolling about the stranger's chair; some crying; some shouting. The mother is pulling at the gown of one, and scolding at another. The visitor, distracted with the noise, endeavors in vain to engage in conversation. The time, and attention, and patience of the parents are absorbed by their lawless family. The visitor, after enduring the uproar for half an hour, is happy in making his escape. Where can there be pleasure, and where can there be profit in such a scene as this?

There are many advantages in encouraging an inquisitive spirit in a child. It has entered upon a world where every thing is new and astonishing. Of course it is hourly meeting with objects upon which it desires information. But as soon as a child finds that his parents encourage him in asking questions, he begins to think that it is a very pretty thing. He will be incessantly presenting his inquiries. His motive will cease to be a gratification of a reasonable and commendable curiosity, and he will desire merely to display his skill, or to talk for the sake of talking. It is very necessary to restrain children in this respect. Their motives are generally distinctly to be seen. And if the motive which prompts the question be improper, let the child receive marks of disapprobation, and not of approval.

"Mother, what is the coffee-pot for?" said a child of three years, at the breakfast table.

"It is to put the coffee in," said the mother.

"And why do you put the coffee in the coffee-pot?"

"Because it is more convenient to pour it out."

"And what," said the child, hesitating and looking around the table to find some new question; "And what—are the cups for?"

"They are to drink from."

"And why do you drink out of the cups?"

In this manner the child, during the whole time allotted for the breakfast, incessantly asked his questions. The mother as continually answered them. She had adopted the principle, that her child must always be encouraged in asking questions. And by blindly and thoughtlessly following out this principle, she was puffing up his heart with vanity, and making him a most unendurable talker. The common sense principle, to guide us upon this subject, is obvious. If the motive be good, and the occasion suitable, let the child be encouraged in his inquiries. If otherwise, let him be discouraged. A child is sitting at the breakfast table with his father and mother. The mother lifts the top of the coffee-pot, and the child observes the contents violently boiling.

"Mother," says the little boy, "what makes the coffee bubble up so?"

Here the motive is good, and the occasion is proper. And one of the parents explains to the child the chemical process which we call the boiling. The parents have reason to be gratified at the observation of the child, and the explanation communicates to him valuable knowledge. But perhaps a stranger is present, with whom the father is engaged in interesting conversation. Under these circumstances, the child asks the same question. It is, however, unseasonable. He ought to be silent when company is present. The mother accordingly replies, "My son, you should not interrupt your father. You must be perfectly silent, and listen to what he is saying."

She does not, however, forget the question, but embraces some opportunity of again alluding to it. She gives him an answer, and shows him that it is very impolite to interrupt the conversation of others, or to engross attention when company is present. Much pleasure is destroyed, and much improvement prevented in permitting the conversation of friends to be interrupted by the loquacity[9] of children.

Some parents, to avoid this inconvenience, immediately send their children from the room when visitors arrive. This is treating children with injustice, and the parents must reap the mortifying consequences in their uncultivated manners and uncultivated minds. Hence, in many gentlemen's families, you find awkward and clownish children. If children are banished from pleasing and intelligent society, they must necessarily grow up rude and ignorant. The course to be pursued, therefore, is plain. They should be often present when friends visit you. But they should be taught to behave properly—to sit in silence and listen. They should not speak unless spoken to. And above all, they should not be thrust forward upon the attention of visitors, to exhibit their attainments, and receive flattery as profusely as your friends may be pleased to deal it out.

---

[9] Loquacity – talkativeness; the habit or practice of talking continually.

3. Do not deceive children. Many are unaware of the evil consequences which result from this common practice. A physician once called to extract a tooth from a child. The little boy seeing the formidable instruments, and anticipating the pain, was exceedingly frightened, and refused to open his mouth. After much fruitless solicitation, the physician said, "Perhaps there is no need of drawing it. Let me rub it a little with my handkerchief, and it may be all that is necessary; it will not hurt you in the least." The boy, trusting his word, opened his mouth. The physician, concealing his instrument in his handkerchief, seized hold of the tooth and wrenched it out. The parents highly applauded his artifice. But the man cheated the child. He abused his confidence; and he inflicted an injury upon his moral feelings not soon to be effaced. Will that physician get his handkerchief into the mouth of the child again? Will he believe what the physician may hereafter say? And when told that it is wicked to say that which is not true, will not the remembrance of the doctor's falsehood be fresh in his mind? And while conscious that his parents approved of the deception, will he not feel it to be right for him to deceive, that he may accomplish his desires? This practice is attended with the most ruinous consequences. It unavoidably teaches the child to despise his parents. After he has detected them in one falsehood, he will not believe them when they speak the truth. It destroys his tenderness of conscience; and it teaches arts of deception. And what are the advantages? Why, in one particular instance, the point is gained.

Let compulsion be resorted to when necessary, but deception never. If a child cannot place implicit confidence in his parent, most assuredly no confidence can be reposed in the child. Is it possible for a mother to practice arts of deception and falsehood, and at the same time her daughter be forming a character of frankness and of truth? Who can for a moment suppose it? We must be what we wish our children to be. They will form their characters from ours.

A mother was once trying to persuade her little son to take some medicine. The medicine was very unpalatable, and she, to induce him to take it, declared it did not taste bad. He did not believe her. He knew, by sad experience, that her word was not to be trusted. A gentleman and friend who was present, took the spoon, and said,

"James, this is medicine, and it tastes very badly. I should not like to take it, but I would, if necessary. You have courage enough to swallow something which does not taste good, have you not?"

"Yes," said James, looking a little less sulky. "But that is very bad indeed."

"I know it," said the gentleman, "I presume you never tasted any thing much worse." The gentleman then tasted the medicine himself, and said, "It is really very unpleasant. But now let us see if you have not resolution enough to take it, bad as it is."

The boy hesitatingly took the spoon.

"It is, really, rather bad," said the gentleman· "but the best way is to summon all your resolution, and down with it at once, like a man."

James made, in reality, a great effort for a child, and swallowed the dose. And who will this child most respect, his deceitful mother, or the honest dealing stranger? And who will he hereafter most readily believe? It ought, however, to be remarked, that had the child been properly governed, he would at once, and without a murmur, have taken what his mother presented. It is certainly, however, a supposable case, that the child might, after all the arguments of the gentleman, still have refused to do his duty. What course should then be pursued? Resort to compulsion, but never to deceit. We cannot deceive our children without seriously injuring them, and destroying our own influence. Frank and open dealing is the only safe policy in family government, as well as on the wider theatre of life. The fraudulent arts and cunning maneuvers of the intriguer are sure, in the end, to promote his own overthrow. Be sincere and honest, and you are safe. The only sure way of securing beneficial results, is by virtuous and honorable means.

4. *Do not be continually finding fault.* It is at times necessary to censure and to punish. But very much may be done by encouraging children when they do well. Be even more careful to express your approbation of good conduct, than your disapprobation of bad. Nothing can more discourage a child than a spirit of incessant faultfinding, on the part of its parent. And hardly any thing can exert a more injurious influence upon the disposition both of the parent and the child. There are two great motives influencing human actions; hope and fear. Both of these are at times necessary. But who would not prefer to have her child influenced to good conduct by the desire of pleasing, rather than by the fear of offending. If a mother never expresses her gratification when her children do well, and is always censuring when she sees any thing amiss, they are discouraged and unhappy. They feel that there is no use in trying to please. Their dispositions become hardened and soured by this ceaseless fretting. At last, finding that, whether

they do well or ill, they are equally found fault with, they relinquish all efforts to please, and become heedless of reproaches.

But let a mother approve of her child's conduct whenever she can. Let her show that his good behavior makes her sincerely happy. Let her reward him for his efforts to please, by smiles and affection. In this way she will cherish in her child's heart some of the noblest and most desirable feelings of our nature. She will cultivate in him an amiable disposition and a cheerful spirit. Your child has been, during the day, very pleasant and obedient. Just before putting him to sleep for the night, you take his hand and say, "My son, you have been a very good boy today. It makes me very happy to see you so kind and obedient. God loves little children who are dutiful to their parents, and he promises to make them happy." This approbation from his mother is, to him, a great reward. And when, with a more than ordinarily affectionate tone, you say, "good night, my dear son," he leaves the room with his little heart full of feeling. And when he closes his eyes for sleep, he is happy, and resolves that he will always try to do his duty.

Basil Hall thus describes the effects produced on board ship, by the different modes of government adopted by different commanders.

"Whenever one of these commanding officers came on board the ship, after an absence of a day or two, and likewise when he made his periodical round of the decks after breakfast, his constant habit was to cast his eye about him, in order to discover what was wrong; to detect the smallest thing that was out of its place; in a word, to find as many grounds for censure as possible. This constituted, in his opinion, the best preventive to neglect, on the part of those under his command; and he acted in this crusty way on principle. The attention of the other officer, on the contrary, appeared to be directed chiefly to those points which he could approve of. For instance he would stop as he went along, from time to time, and say to the first lieutenant, 'Now, these ropes are very nicely arranged; this mode of stowing the men's bags and mess kids is just as I wish to see it;' while the officer first described would not only pass by these well-arranged things, which had cost hours of labor to put in order, quite unnoticed, but would not be easy till his eye had caught hold of some casual omission which afforded an opening for disapprobation.

"One of these captains would remark to the first lieutenant, as he walked along, 'How white and clean you have got the decks today! I think you must have been at them all the morning, to have got them into such order.' The other, in similar circumstances, but eager to find fault, would say, even if the decks were as white and clean as drifted snow, 'I wish you would teach these sweepers to clear away that bundle of shakings!' pointing to a bit of rope-yarn, not half an inch long, left under the trunk of a gun. It seemed, in short, as if nothing was more vexatious to one of these officers, than to discover things so correct as to afford him no good opportunity for finding fault; while, to the other, the necessity of censuring really appeared a punishment to himself.

"Under the one, accordingly, we all worked with cheerfulness, from a conviction that nothing we did in a proper way would miss approbation.

"But our duty under the other, being performed in fear, seldom went on with much spirit. We had no personal satisfaction in doing things correctly, from the certainty of getting no commendation.

"The great chance, also, of being censured, even in those cases where we had labored most industriously to merit approbation, broke the spring of all generous exertion, and by teaching us to anticipate blame as a matter of course, defeated the very purpose of punishment when it fell upon us. The case being quite hopeless, the chastisement seldom conduced either to the amendment of an offender, or to the prevention of offences. But what seemed the oddest thing of all was, that these men were both as kindhearted as could be; or, if there were any difference, the fault-finder was the better natured, and, in matters not professional, the more indulgent of the two.

"The line of conduct I have described was purely a matter of official system, not at all of feeling. Yet, as it then appeared, and still appears to me, nothing could be more completely erroneous than the snarling method of the one, or more decidedly calculated to do good than the approving style of the other. It has, in fact, always appeared to me an absurdity, to make any real distinction between public and private matters in these respects.

"Nor is there the smallest reason why the same principle of civility, or consideration, or by whatever name that quality be called, by which the feelings of others are consulted, should not modify professional intercourse quite as much as it does that of the freest society, without any risk that the requisite strictness of discipline would be hurt by an attention to good manners.

"The desire of discovering that things are right and a sincere wish to express our approbation, are habits which, in almost every situation in life, have the best possible effects in practice.

"They are vastly more agreeable certainly to the superior himself, whether he be the colonel of a regiment, the captain of a ship, or the head of a house; for the mere act of approving seldom fails to put a man's thoughts into that pleasant train which predisposes him to be habitually pleased, and this frame of mind alone, essentially helps the propagation of a similar cheerfulness amongst all those who are about him. It requires, indeed, but a very little experience of soldiers or sailors, children, servants, or any other kind of dependents, or even of companions and superiors, to show that this good humor, on the part of those whom we wish to influence, is the best possible coadjutor[10] to our schemes of management, whatever these may be."

The judicious exercise of approbation is of the first importance in promoting obedience, and in cultivating in the bosom of your child affectionate and cheerful feelings. Let your smiles animate your boy's heart, and cheer him on in duty. When he returns from school, with his clothes clean and his countenance happy, reward him with the manifestation of a mother's love. This will be the strongest incentive to neatness and care. An English gentleman used to encourage his little children to early rising, by calling the one who first made her appearance in the parlor in the morning, Lark. The early riser was addressed by that name during the day. This slight expression of parental approval was found sufficient to call up all the children to the early enjoyment of the morning air. A child of ten makes a very great effort to do something to merit a smile from its mother. And most bitter tears are frequently shed because parents do not sufficiently sympathize in these feelings.

---

[10] Coadjutor – one who aids another; an assistant; a fellow-helper; associate.

The enjoyment of many a social circle, and the disposition of many an affectionate child, are spoiled by unceasing complaints. Some persons get into such a habit of finding fault that it becomes as natural to them as to breathe. Nothing pleases them. In every action, and in every event, they are searching for something to disapprove. Like venomous reptiles, they have the faculty of extracting poison from the choicest blessings. Children are, very much, creatures of sympathy. They form their characters from those around them. And we must cherish in our own bosoms those virtues we would foster in theirs. If we would give them calm and gentle and friendly feelings, we must first show them, by our own example, how valuable those feelings are.

5. Never punish by exciting imaginary fears. There is something very remarkable in the universal prevalence of superstition. Hardly an individual is to be found, enlightened or unenlightened, who is not, in a greater or less degree, under the influence of these irrational fears. There is, in the very nature of man, a strong susceptibility of impression upon this subject. A ghost story will be listened to with an intensity of interest which hardly any thing else can awaken. Persons having the care of children, not infrequently take advantage of this, and endeavor to amuse by relating these stories, or to govern by exciting their fears. It surely is not necessary to argue the impropriety of such a course. Every one knows how ruinous must be the result. Few parents, however, practice the caution which is necessary to prevent others from filling the minds of their children with superstition. How often do we find persons who retain through life the influence which has thus been exerted upon them in childhood. It becomes to them a real calamity. Much watchfulness is required to preserve the mind from such injuries.

There is a mode of punishment, not infrequent, which is very reprehensible. A child is shut up in the cellar, or in a dark closet. It is thus led to associate ideas of terror with darkness. This effect has sometimes been so powerful, that hardly any motive would induce a child to go alone into a dark room. And sometimes even they fear, after they have retired for sleep, to be left alone without a light. But there is no difficulty in training up children to be as fearless by night as by day. And you can find many who do not even dream of danger in going any where about the house in the darkest night. If you would cultivate this state of mind in your children, it is necessary that you should preserve them from ideas of supernatural appearances, and should never appeal to imaginary fears. Train up your children to be virtuous and fearless. Moral courage is one of the surest safeguards of virtue.

An English writer gives a most appalling account of two instances in which fatal consequences attended the strong excitement of fear. Says he, "I knew in Philadelphia, as fine, and as sprightly, and as intelligent a child as ever was born, made an idiot for life, by being, when about three years old, shut into a dark closet by a maid-servant, in order to terrify it into silence. The thoughtless creature first menaced it with sending it to *'the bad place;'* and at last, to reduce it to silence, put it into the closet, shut the door, and went out of the room. She went back in a few minutes, and found the child in a *fit*. It recovered from that, but was for life an idiot. When the parents, who had been out two days and two nights on a visit of pleasure, came home, they were told that the child had had *a fit*, but they were not told the cause. The girl, however, who was a neighbor's daughter, being on her death-bed about ten years afterwards, could not die in peace without sending for the mother of the child and asking forgiveness of her. Thousands upon thousands of human beings have been deprived of their senses by these and similar means.

"It is not long ago that we read, in the newspapers, of a child being absolutely *killed* (at Birmingham [England], I think) by being thus frightened. The parents had gone out into what is called an evening party. The servants, naturally enough, had their party at home; and the mistress, who, by some unexpected accident, had been brought home at an early hour, finding the parlor full of company, ran up stairs to see about her child, about two or three years old. She found it with its eyes open, but *fixed!* touching it, she found it inanimate. The doctor was sent for in vain: it was dead. The maid pretended to know nothing of the cause; but some one of the parties assembled discovered, pinned up to the curtains of the bed, *a horrid figure,* made up partly of a frightful mask! This, as the wretched girl confessed, had been done to keep the child *quiet* while she was with her company below. When one reflects on the anguish that the poor little thing must have endured before the life was quite frightened out of it, one can find no terms sufficiently strong to express the abhorrence due to the perpetrator of this crime, which was, in fact, a cruel murder; and, if it was beyond the reach of the law, it was so, and is so, because, as in the cases of parricide,[11] the law, in making no provision for punishment peculiarly severe, has, out of respect to human nature, supposed such crimes to be *impossible.*"

---

[11] Parricide – a person who murders his father or mother.

I have in this chapter alluded to some of the most common and prominent faults in education. They cannot all, however, be particularly mentioned. The faithful mother must have continually a watchful eye; she must observe the *effect* of her own practices. She must carefully search out every little defect and trifling error. We must think and observe for ourselves. It is in vain to hope to make attainment in any thing valuable without effort. The views of others may be of essential aid in laying down general principles, in exciting our own thoughts, and in stimulating us to resolution and fidelity. But, after all, unless we are willing to think ourselves; to study the dispositions of our children; to watch the influence of the various motives we present to their minds, many faults will pass undetected, and we shall lose many advantages we might otherwise have obtained.

CHAPTER SIX

Religious Instruction: Part I

Very great success has attended the efforts which have been
made to collect children in Sabbath schools for religious
instruction. Maternal associations have been of inestimable
value. But nothing can supersede the necessity of effort and instruction at the fire-side. The mother must collect her little
flock around her and take upon herself the responsibility of
their religious education. She may find enjoyment and
improvement in associating with others for prayer; and if she be
faithful, she will see that her children are punctual attendants of
the Sabbath school. But she will not regard these as exonerating
herself in the least degree from responsibility. The influence of
Sabbath schools has undoubtedly been to awaken more general
interest at home in behalf of the spiritual welfare of children.
Still there is danger that some parents may feel that the
responsibility is transferred from themselves to the Sabbath
school teachers; and that they accomplish their duty in seeing
them punctually at school with their lessons well committed.

1. *It is, however, of the first importance that home should be the
sanctuary of religious instruction.* The mother must be the earnest
and affectionate guide to the Savior. She must take her little
ones by the hand and lead them in the paths of piety.

No one else can possibly have the influence which a mother may possess, or the facilities which she enjoys. She knows the various dispositions of her children; their habits of thought; their moods of mind. Thus can she adapt instruction to their needs. She alone can improve the numberless occurrences which open the mind for instruction, and give it susceptibility to religious impression. She is with them when they are in sickness or pain. She can take advantage of the calm of the morning, and of the solemn stillness of the evening. In moments of sadness she can point their minds to brighter worlds, and to more satisfying joys. God has conferred upon the mother advantages which no one else can possess. With these advantages he has connected responsibilities which cannot be laid aside, or transferred to another. At home, and by the parents, the great duty of religious education must be faithfully performed. The quiet fire-side is the most sacred sanctuary; maternal affection is the most eloquent pleader, and an obedient child is the most promising subject of religious impressions. Let mothers feel this as they ought, and they will seldom see their children leave the paternal roof unfortified with Christian principles and sincere piety.

2. *Parents must have deep devotional feelings themselves.* It is certainly vain to hope that you can induce your children to fix their affections upon another world, while yours are fixed upon this. Your example will counteract all the influence of your instructions. Unless Christian feelings animate your heart, it is folly to expect that you can instill those principles into the hearts of your children. They will imitate your example. They confide in your guidance. That little child which God has given you, and which is so happy in your affection, feels safe in

cherishing those feelings which it sees you are cherishing. And, mother! can you look upon your confiding child and witness all her fond endearments and warm embraces, and not feel remorse in the consciousness that your example is leading her away from God, and consigning her to ceaseless sorrow?

You love your child. Your child loves you, and cannot dream that you are abusing its confidence, and leading it in the paths of sin and destruction. How would it be shocked in being told that its mother is the cruel betrayer of its eternal happiness! You are wedded to the world. You have not given your heart to God. Not content with being the destroyer of your own soul, you must carry with you to the world of woe, the child who loves you as its mother and its friend. O there is an aggravation of cruelty in this which cannot be described. One would think that every smile would disturb your peace; that every proof of affection would pierce your heart; that remorse would keep you awake at midnight, and embitter every hour. The murderer of the body can scarce withstand the stings of conscience. But, O unchristian mother! You are the destroyer of the soul. And of whose soul? The soul of your own confiding child. We cannot speak less plainly on this topic. We plead the unparalleled wrongs of children, betrayed by a mother's smile and a mother's kiss. Satan led Adam from Paradise. Judas betrayed his Master. But here we see a mother leading her child, her own immortal child, far from God and peace, to the rebellion of worldliness and the storms of retribution. That little child fol-lowing in your footsteps, is the heir of eternity. It is to survive the lapse of all coming years; to emerge from the corruptions of the grave; to expand in spiritual existence, soaring in the angel's lofty flight, or groping in the demon's gloom. Thou, O mother!

art its guide to immortality; to heaven's green pastures, or to despair's dreary wastes. If you go on in unrepented sin, your child, in all probability, will go with you.

We have heard of a child, upon her dying bed, raising her eyes to her parents and exclaiming, in bitterness of spirit, "O my parents! you never told me of death, or urged me to prepare for it; and now," said she, bursting into an agony of tears, "I am dying, and my soul is lost." She died. Her sun went down in darkness. What were the feelings of those parents! What agony must have rent their bosoms! How must the specter of their ruined daughter pursue them in all the employments of the day, and disturb their slumbers by night. But you must meet your children again. The trump of judgment will summon you to the bar of Christ. How fruitless would be the attempt to describe your feelings there!

> "That awful day will surely come;
> The appointed hour makes haste."

Death is succeeded by judgment and judgment by eternity. If you are the destroyer of your child, through eternity you must bear its reproaches. You must gaze upon the wreck of its immortal spirit, while conscience says that, if you had been faithful, you and your child might have been reposing in heaven. Think not that you can go in one path, and induce your child to walk in another. You must not only "point to heaven," but "lead the way." The first thing to be done is for a mother to give her own heart to God. Become a Christian yourself, and then you may hope for God's blessing upon your efforts to lead your child to the Savior. We do entreat every mother who reads these pages, as she values her own happiness and the happiness of her children, immediately to surrender her heart to God.

Atoning blood has removed every difficulty from the way. The Holy Spirit is ready, in answer to your prayers, to grant you all needful assistance. Every hour that you neglect this duty, you are leading your children farther from God, and rendering the prospect of their return more hopeless.

3. Present religion in a cheerful aspect. There is no real enjoyment without piety. The tendency of religion is to make us happy here and hereafter; to divest the mind of gloom, and fill it with joy. Many parents err in this respect. They dwell too much upon the terrors of the law. They speak with countenances saddened and gloomy. Religion becomes to the child an unwelcome topic, and is regarded as destructive of happiness. The idea of God is associated with gloom and terror. Many parents have, in their latter years, become convinced of the injudicious course they have pursued in this respect. They have so connected religious considerations with melancholy countenances and mournful tones of voice, as to cause the subject to be unnecessarily repugnant.

We may, indeed, err upon the other extreme. The nature of sin, and the justice of God, and the awful penalty of his law, should be distinctly exhibited. The child should be taught to regard God as that being who, while he loves his creatures, cannot look upon sin but with abhorrence. If we speak to children simply of the Creator's goodness, as manifested in the favors we are daily receiving, an erroneous impression of God's character will be conveyed. It is to be feared that many deceive themselves in thinking they love God. They have in their minds a poetic idea of an amiable and sentimental being, whose character is composed of fondness and indulgence. Such persons are as far from worshipping the true God, as is the

Indian devotee or the sensual Moslem. God must be represented as he has exhibited himself to us in the Bible and in the works of nature. He is a God of mercy and of justice. He is a God of love, and a consuming fire. He is to be regarded with our warmest affections, and also with reverence and godly fear. Let, therefore, children distinctly understand that sin cannot pass unpunished. But it should also be understood that judgment is God's strange work. Ordinarily speak of his goodness. Show his readiness to forgive. Excite the gratitude of the child by speaking of the joys of heaven. Thus let the duties of religion ever be connected with feelings of enjoyment and images of happiness, that the child may perceive that gloom and sorrow are connected only with disobedience and irreligion. There is enough in the promised joys of heaven to rouse a child's most animated feelings. This subject has more to cheer the youthful heart than any other which can be presented. Appeal to gratitude. Excite hope. Speak of the promised reward. Thus may you most reasonably hope to lead your child to love its Maker, and to live for heaven. Reserve the terrors of the law for solemn occasions, when you may produce a deep and abiding impression. If you are continually introducing these motives, the mind becomes hardened against their influence; religion becomes a disagreeable topic, and the inveteracy of sin is confirmed.

4. *Improve appropriate occasions.* We all know that there are times when there is peculiar tenderness of conscience and susceptibility of impression. These changes come over the mind, sometimes from unaccountable causes. One day the Christian will feel a warmth of devotional feeling and elevation of spiritual enjoyment, which the next day he in vain endeavors

to attain. The man whose affections are fixed upon the world, at one time will be almost satisfied with the pleasure he is gathering. The world looks bright; hope is animated; and he rushes on with new vigor in his delusive pursuits. The next day all his objects of desire appear as perfect shadows. He feels the heartlessness of his pleasures; his spirit is sad within him; and he is almost resolved to be a Christian. With these changes nearly all are familiar. Sometimes they may be accounted for from known external causes. At other times the causes elude our search.

A mother should ever be watchful to improve such occasions. When she sees her child with an unusually tender spirit, with a pensive countenance and subdued feelings—let her then look to God in fervent prayer, and with all the persuasions of a mother's love endeavor to guide her child to the Savior. When the mind is in such a state as this, it is prepared for religious instruction. It then can be made to feel how heartless are all joys but those of piety. Its hold upon the world is loosened, and it may more easily be led to wander in those illimitable regions where it may hereafter find its home. O how sweet a pleasure it is to present the joys of religion to a child whose feelings are thus chastened; to behold the tear of feeling moistening its eye; to see its little bosom heaving with the new emotions which are rising there! If there be a joy on earth, it is to be found in such a scene as this. The happy mother thus guiding her young immortal to its heavenly home, experiences a rapture of feeling which the world knoweth not of. Such occasions are not infrequently arising, and the mother should endeavor always to have her heart warm with love to Christ, that in such an hour she may communicate its warmth to the bosom of her child.

There are certain seasons also which are peculiarly appropriate for guiding the thoughts to heaven. Our feelings vary with scenes around us. Upon some dark and tempestuous night you lead your little son to his chamber. The rain beats violently upon the windows. The wind whistles around the corners of the dwelling. All without is darkness and gloom. The mind of the child is necessarily affected by this rage of the elements. You embrace the opportunity to inculcate a lesson of trust in God "My son," you say, "it is God who causes this wind to blow, and the rain to fall. Neither your father nor I can cause the storm to cease, or increase its violence. If God wished, he could make the wind blow with such fury as to beat in all the windows and destroy the house. But God will take care of you, my son, if you sincerely ask him. No one else can take care of you. I hope that you will pray that God will protect you, and your father, and me, tonight. When God commands, the storm will cease. The clouds will disappear; all will be calm. And the bright moon and twinkling stars will shine out again."

In some such manner as this the child may be taught his entire dependence upon God. He cannot fail of obtaining a deep impression of the power of his Maker. You may say that God is omnipotent, and it will produce but a feeble impression. But point to some actual exhibition of God's power, and the attention is arrested, and the truth is felt. When the mother leaves the room, and her son remains alone and in darkness, listening to the roar of the storm, will not his mind be expanded with new ideas of the greatness and the power of his Maker? Will he not feel that it is a fearful thing to offend such a being? And if he has been rightly instructed to place his trust in God, the agitation of the elements will not trouble the serenity of his heart. He will feel that with God for his protector, he need fear no evil. Some such simple occurrence as this may often be improved to produce an impression which never can be forgotten. Such thoughts as these, introduced to the mind of a child, will enlarge its capacities, give it maturity, lead it to reflection, and, by the blessing of God, promote its eternal well-being. One such transient incident has a greater effect than hours of ordinary religious conversation.

One of the most important duties of the mother is to *watch for these occasions and diligently to improve them.* Any parent who is faithful will find innumerable opportunities, which will enable her to come into almost immediate contact with the heart of her child. The hour of sickness comes. Your little daughter is feverish and restless upon her pillow. You bathe her burning brow and moisten her parched tongue, and she hears your prayer that she may be restored to health. At length the fever subsides. She awakes from refreshing sleep, relieved from pain. You tell her then, that if God had not interposed, her sickness would have increased till she had died. By pointing her attention to this one act of kindness in God, which she can see and feel, you may excite emotions of sincere gratitude. You may thus lead her to real grief that she should ever disobey her heavenly Father.

A child in the neighborhood dies. Your daughter accompanies you to the funeral. She looks upon the lifeless corpse of her little companion. And shall a mother neglect such an opportunity to teach her child the meaning of death? When your daughter retires to sleep at night, she will most certainly think of her friend who has died. As you speak to her of the eternal world to which her friend has gone—of the judgment-seat of Christ—of the new scenes of joy or woe upon which she has entered, will not her youthful heart feel? And will not tears of sympathy fill her eyes? And as you tell your daughter that she too soon must die; leave all her friends; appear before Christ to be judged; and enter upon eternal existence; will not the occurrence of the day give a reality and an effect to your remarks which will long be remembered? There are few children who can resist such appeals. The Savior, who took little children in his arms and blessed them, will not despise this day of small things, but will cherish the feelings thus excited, and strengthen the feeble resolve. We have every encouragement to believe that God, who is more ready to give his Holy Spirit to them that ask him, than a mother to feed her hungry child, will accompany these efforts with his blessing.

A father once led his little daughter into the grave-yard, to show her the grave of a playmate, who, a few days before, had been consigned to her cold and narrow bed. The little girl looked for some moments in silence and sadness upon the fresh mound, and then looking up, said "Papa, I now know what is meant by the hymn,

'I, in the burying place, may see,
Graves shorter there than I.'

"My grave would be longer than this." This dear little child now lies by the side of that grave. But her parents can smile through their tears, as they believe that her spirit is in heaven. It is by introducing children to such scenes, and seizing upon such occasions, that we may most successfully inculcate lessons of piety. One such incident enters more deeply into the heart than volumes of ordinary conversation.

child is angry. His flushed cheek and violent motions show the sinful irritation of his mind. Shall the mother now converse with him upon the wickedness of these feelings and God's displeasure? No! It is unseasonable. It would be as unavailing as to converse with a madman, or one intoxicated. Punish him for his irritation in some way which will soothe his feelings and lead him to reflection. But wait till these passions have subsided before you attempt to reason with him upon their impropriety, and to lead him to evangelical repentance.[12] Kneel by his bed-side in the silence of his chamber, and in the pensive hour of evening. When his mind is calm, and passion is not triumphing over reason, he will hear you, and may be melted to contrition. When Peter denied his Master, he did it with cursing and swearing. But when his fears had subsided, and the hour of reflection came, with a sad heart he entered the hall of Pilate. Then did a single glance from the Savior pierce his heart, "and he went out and wept bitterly."

A child is highly excited with pleasurable emotions. His attention is so highly engrossed by the immediate object of his enjoyment, that it is almost impossible to draw his thoughts to any other subject. If, under these circumstances, an effort is made to convince him of the uncertainty of human enjoyments, of his own sinfulness, of the need of a Savior, the effort will not only, in all probability, be unavailing, but the subject will be so unwelcome as to excite disgust. There are times when the mind is prepared with gratitude to receive religious instruction. Let

---

[12] Evangelical Repentance – is perhaps best summarized in the 17th century catechism answer: "Repentance unto life is a saving grace, whereby a sinner, out of a true sense of his sin, and apprehension of the mercy of God in Christ, doth, with grief and hatred of his sin, turn from it unto God, with full purpose of, and endeavor after, new obedience."

such be improved. There are others when the mind is so manifestly engrossed in one all-absorbing subject that it is in vain to present any other. If you would not connect religion with unpleasant associations, and excite repugnance, do not on such occasions obtrude this subject.

If a hunter should enter a forest and walk along loading and firing at random, he might accidentally get some game, but most assuredly he would frighten away far more than he would secure. If a parent, with blind and unthinking zeal, is incessantly throwing out random remarks, she may by chance produce the desired effect. She will however more frequently excite opposition, and confirm rebellion, than lead to penitence and prayer.

Guard against long and tedious conversations. The mind of a child cannot be fixed for any great length of time upon one subject without exhaustion. Every word that is uttered, after there are manifestations of weariness, will do more harm than good. If a mother will exercise her own judgment, and gather wisdom from her own observation, she will soon acquire that facility in adapting her instructions which will have the best tendency to improve her child. No rules can supersede the necessity of personal watchfulness and reflection.

CHAPTER SEVEN

Religious Instruction: Part II

The views which are generally entertained of heaven are far more indefinite than they need be. This home of the blest is described in the Bible with the most magnificent imagery nature affords. Heaven is spoken of as having a distinct locality, just as much as is London or Paris, or any place on earth. We hear of the splendor of the golden city, adorned with every beauty with which the hand of Omnipotence can embellish it; of the mansions glittering with architectural magnificence. We are informed of the social enjoyments of that world. The Christian is introduced to the society of angels; converses with them; unites in their enjoyments; becomes a loved member of their happy community. We are informed of the active delights of heaven. Angel bands fly to and fro, the rejoicing messengers of God. They unfold their wings and take their rapid flight where all the glories of the universe allure their curiosity, and where no darkness succeeds the splendor of ceaseless day. The joys of sense are described. The eye gazes full and undazzled upon the brightness of God's throne. The ear is charmed with melody. The body of the Christian is to arise from the grave, incorruptible and immortal. There is the union of soul and body in that happy world. There we meet our Christian friends; recognize them; rejoice in their love. Thus we pass our eternity with songs, and everlasting joy upon our heads, where sorrow and sighing for ever flee away.

How vivid and impressive are the views which the pen of inspiration gives of the Christian's future abode! Yet the very common idea entertained of heaven is, that it is a vast aerial expanse, where shadowy and unsubstantial spirits repose in mysterious and indefinable enjoyment. There is, indeed, with many individuals, an impression that it is almost wicked to associate ideas of joys with which we now are familiar with that celestial abode. But is it not safe, is it not a duty, to be guided in our instructions by the Bible? Admitting that the descriptions of the Bible are figurative, as they of necessity must be, still these are the figures which God has employed to convey to our minds an idea of the joys of heaven. And God would surely select the most appropriate figures and those which most nearly resemble the enjoyments to be illustrated.

1. *Therefore it is our privilege and our duty to describe heaven to our children, as God has described it to us.* Thus may we give it vividness in their minds. Thus may we excite in their youthful bosoms the most intense desire to enter that happy world. And why has God unfolded its glories but to allure to holiness and entice us home? Your son has an unusual thirst for knowledge. His curiosity is ever on the alert. He is prying into nature's mysterious movements, and asking questions which the human mind cannot answer. Tell him that there are no limits to human improvements; that the grave cannot enchain the energies of mind; that time cannot circumscribe its range; that eternity cannot weary its bowers; that it will advance in its acquisitions,

and soar in its flight, long after suns, and moons, and stars shall have waxed old and decayed. Tell him that in heaven he shall understand all the wonders of God's works, and experience the most exquisite delight, as he looks into and comprehends all the machinery of nature. And then you can tell him of the Savior, who died that he might introduce him to this happy world. Your daughter has an ear charmed with the melody of sound. Music is to her a source of exquisite enjoyment. Is there no music in heaven? Is there no melody in the "chorus of the skies?" Is there nothing enrapturing to the soul while uniting with angel bands in their hallelujahs? God has thus described heaven to us. Why should we not then animate our children with the same description? You may, in familiar language, carry the thoughts of your daughter away to companies of happy angels, with celestial harps and divine voices rolling their notes of joy through heaven's wide concave. Thus will she have some definite idea of the enjoyments to which she is invited. The joys of heaven will be to her intensely alluring; and she will be led to inquire more earnestly into the way of salvation, and with more fervor to implore God's aid to overcome sin and prepare her for a heavenly home.

Your child has an affectionate disposition, a heart open to receive friendship, and to pour forth its love. Tell him of the love of heaven, of God, of the angels. Tell him of the love which animates the bosoms of those noble spirits who have not a single fault to repel attachment. Tell him of again meeting all his friends who love the Savior, in that world where an unkind word, or an unkind look, or an unkind thought, is unknown. And as you dwell upon the proofs of a Savior's love, his heart may be melted.

Is your child passionately fond of nature's scenery? Does he look with a poet's eye upon the ocean, upon the starry canopy, upon the gilded clouds of sunset? There surely is magnificence in the scenery of heaven. There is splendor worth beholding in the visions of angels, the throne of God, the widespread universe of countless worlds. What is the ocean but a drop sprinkled from the almighty hand? What is Niagara, to us so magnificent, but a tiny rivulet rippling over its pebbly channel? Animate your child with the description of those glories of heaven, before which all the sublimity of earth sinks to insignificance. Fear not that this will extinguish in his bosom a taste for nature's beauties. It will, while increasing the enjoyment he derives from these sources, refine and elevate his mind, and give him ardent desires to be prepared for this world of glory. Fear not that this will strengthen in his heart the principles of selfishness instead of leading him to piety. If God had felt such fears, he never would have presented us the allurements of heaven, or the terrors of hell. Present these joys, that your child may be induced by them to repent of sin, to trust in the Savior, and to consecrate life to his service.

These descriptions are necessarily in some degree figurative, and we must so instruct our children. But we must not neglect the use of these figures, for they convey to the mind the most correct conception that can be attained of the enjoyment of the future world. The fact that God has selected them proves that no other language can be equally appropriate. They describe, as perfectly as human language can describe, the nature of heaven's enjoyments. But they do not come up to the reality; for eye hath not seen, nor ear heard, nor human heart conceived, the joys which God has prepared for those who love him.

God knows how to adapt instruction to the human mind. We must imitate his example. And we must present heaven to our children as God has presented it to us, crowded with images of delight. The purest and noblest joys we experience on earth will be found again in that world, only infinitely elevated and refined. And he must adopt singular principles of interpretation, who does not read in the Bible, that in heaven we shall find splendor of scenery, harmony of music, congeniality of companions, ardor of love, delight of active motion, mansions of glory, and homes of never-failing bliss. Let us urge these views upon our children till their hearts are warmed by them. Nothing can have a stronger tendency to convince of the folly of laying up treasures upon earth. And this will lead them to listen with interest, to learn how salvation is to be obtained.

2. Dwell particularly upon the Savior. The Scriptures declare that the preaching of Christ crucified is the powerful instrument which God uses in convincing of sin, and leading to penitence and gratitude. And the history of the church in all ages has shown that the history of a Savior' love and death will awaken contrition and melt the heart, when all other appeals are in vain. Your child will listen, with tearful eye, while you tell of the Savior's elevation in heaven; of his becoming man; of the sufferings and persecution of his life; and of his cruel death upon the cross. And when you tell your child that it was God who thus became manifest in the flesh, and suffered these indignities that he might redeem his sinful creatures from woe, you will convey to the tender mind such an idea of God's kindness, and the ingratitude of sinners, as nothing else can produce. The philosopher may admire the noble conception of the eternal, incomprehensible, invisible Spirit. But it is God, as manifested in the compassionate, gentle, and suffering Savior, who attracts the sympathies of the heart. A definite idea is introduced to the youthful mind when you speak of him who took little children in his arms and blessed them. Every Christian can judge, from the effect produced upon his own heart by the recital of a Savior's love, of the tendency it has to awaken in the bosom of a child the deepest emotions of contrition and gratitude. It is very observable, in all the accounts of youthful piety, that the Savior is the prominent object of affection.

Any person will be interested, in turning over the pages of almost any pious child's biography, to witness how strong the impression which a Savior's love produces upon the heart. Even under the most adverse circumstances, the youthful heart has found its way to him. Not a few instances have occurred, in which parents, who have not been accustomed to give prominence to the Savior in their instructions, have been surprised to find that Jesus Christ is the sympathizing friend to whom a child, in sickness and in suffering, has most affectionately clung. God, in Christ, has attractions which nothing else can have.

When little Nathan Dickerman[13] was asked, "What do you love to think about most when you are in pain?"

"The Lord Jesus Christ," he answered.

At another time his biographer records, "Nathan is very sick tonight. His heart is beating most violently and rapidly,

---

[13] Nathan W. Dickerman (1822-1830) was from Boston, MA. He came to a saving knowledge of Jesus Christ at an early age, and died when he as just eight. His story was told in the book *Memoir of Nathan W. Dickerman* published by The American Tract Society in 1831. Solid Ground may reprint this little gem.

while the pulse can hardly he perceived at the wrist. But he says he is more happy than usual. I asked him why. He replied,

'Because my Savior is nearer.'

"Being asked which was his favorite hymn; he thought a moment, and repeated,

> 'One there is above all others
> Well deserves the name of friend;
> His is love beyond a brother's,
> Costly, free, and knows no end.
>
> Which of all our friends, to save us,
> Could or would have shed his blood?
> But this Savior died to have us
> Reconciled in him to God.'

The remembrance of what the Savior suffered sustained him in all his sufferings. Redeeming love was the theme of his sweetest meditations.

"One day, some one was mentioning in the room, that his disease was of such a nature that he would probably die suddenly. Nathan heard it, and rising up in the bed, clasped his hands together, and repeated the verse,

> 'Jesus can make a dying bed
> Feel soft as downy pillows are,
> While on his breast I lean my head,
> And breathe my soul out sweetly there.'

"And after sitting a few moments in silence, he added another:

> 'Jesus, my God, I know his name
> His name is all my trust;
> Nor will he put my soul to shame
> Nor let my hope be lost.'

Isn't that a good hope, Ma?' he said.

We might open to almost any memoir of early piety, in illustration of this principle. And indeed every one who is familiar with the characteristics of devotional feeling, as they are exemplified in the mind of a child, must have observed the wonderful adaptation of religious truth to our weakness and frailty.

Let parents, therefore, imitate the apostles, and preach to their children a suffering Savior. Show them God in Christ, reconciling the world to himself. This is the simplicity of the Gospel. Indeed, we can hardly conceive it possible for the affections of a child to cling with ardor to any object, of which it cannot form some definite conception. Tell your child of Christ, who created him; of Christ, who became man, and suffered and died to save him; of Christ, before whose judgment-seat he soon must appear; of Christ, whose praises the Christian will sing in heaven, ages without end. Thus is God, if I may so express it, *simplified* to the comprehension of the child. The mother who does not often present this Savior, and dwell upon the story of his sufferings and death, has not yet learnt the simplicity and power of the Gospel. All other motives are feeble, compared with this. You may search the world of fact and of imagination in vain for any motive calculated to produce so deep an impression upon the mind. And every thing in this astonishing occurrence has a tendency to promote humility, and penitence, and love. I dwell the more earnestly upon this point, for it appears to me of primary importance. It is the all-availing instrument which God has given to subdue the power of sin in the heart.

3. Pray with your children. It is not only the duty of a mother to pray *for* her children, but when they are young, to pray *with* them. Let them hear your fervent supplications that God will make them his friends. Let them see that your desires are intense that they may be preserved from sin, and prepared for heaven. The feelings which animate the bosom of the mother will, by sympathy, in some degree, be transferred to the bosoms of the children. These scenes of devotion will long be remembered. And if your efforts and your prayers are not answered with the early evidences of your children's piety, these hours of devotion will leave a trace upon the memory never to be effaced. Through all succeeding years they will operate as restraints from plunging into guilty excess, and as monitions of conscience calling loudly to repentance and virtue.

It is reported of a man, eminent for his talents, his elevated situation in life, and his dissipation, that one evening, while sitting at the gambling-table, he was observed to be unusually sad. His associates rallied him upon his serious aspect. He endeavored, by rousing himself, and by sallies of wit, which he had always at command, to turn away their attention, and throw off the transient gloom. Not many moments transpired before he seemed again lost in thought, and dejected, by some mournful contemplations. This exposed him so entirely to the ridicule of his companions, that he could not defend himself. As they poured in upon him their taunts and jeers, he at last remarked, "Well, to tell the truth, I cannot help thinking, every now and then, of the prayers my mother used to offer for me at my bedside when I was a child. Old as I am, I cannot forget the impressions of those early years." Here was a man of highly cultivated mind, and of talents of so high an order as to give him influence and eminence, notwithstanding his dissolute life, and yet neither lapse of years, nor acquisitions of knowledge, nor crowding cares, nor scenes of dissipation, could obliterate the effect which a mother's devotions had left upon his mind. The still small voice of a mother's prayers rose above the noise of guilty revelry. The pious mother, though dead, still continued to speak in impressive rebuke to her dissolute son. Many facts might be introduced illustrating the importance of this duty. The following is so much to the point, and affords such cheering encouragement, that I cannot refrain from relating it.

A few years ago, a gentleman from England brought a letter of introduction to a gentleman in this country. The stranger was of accomplished mind and manners, but in sentiment an infidel. The gentleman to whom he brought letters of introduction, and his lady, were active Christian philanthropists. They invited the stranger to make their house his home, and treated him with every possible attention. Upon the evening of his arrival, just before the usual hour for retiring, the gentleman, knowing the peculiarity of his guest's sentiments, observed to him that the hour had arrived in which they usually attended family prayers; that he should be happy to have him remain and unite with them, or, if he preferred, he could retire. The gentleman intimated that it would give him pleasure to remain. A chapter of the Bible was read, and the family all knelt in prayer, the stranger with the rest. In a few days the stranger left this hospitable dwelling, and embarked on board a ship for a foreign land. In the course of three or four years, however, the providence of God again led that stranger to the same dwelling. But O how changed! He came the happy Christian, the humble man of piety and prayer. In the course of the evening's conversation he remarked that when he, on the first evening of his previous visit, knelt with them in family prayer, it was the first time for many years that he had bowed the knee to his Maker. This act brought to his mind such a crowd of recollections, it so vividly reminded him of a parent's prayers which he had heard at home, that it completely absorbed his attention. His emotion was so great that he did not hear one syllable of the prayer which was uttered, from its commencement to its close. And God made this the instrument of leading him from the dreary wilds of infidelity to the peace and the joy of piety. His parents, I believe, had long before gone home to their rest; but the prayers they had offered for and with their son, had left an influence which could not die. They might have prayed ever so fervently *for* him, but if they had not prayed *with* him, if they had not knelt by his side and caused his listening ear to hear their earnest supplications, their child might have continued through life unreconciled to his Maker.

There is efficacy in prayer. God hears and answers our requests. But he does this in accordance with the laws which he has established. It is presumption to expect that he will interrupt the harmony of those laws. He acts through them. And we should endeavor to accommodate all our efforts to the known habits of mind; to present those motives which have a tendency to influence. God answered the prayers of these pious parents; but he did it through the instrumentality of the very effort they were making in asking him to bless their son.

4. *Teach your children to pray themselves.* It may be very useful to teach a child the Lord's prayer and other simple forms. And a child may thus really pray—give utterance to his own feelings in the language of another. But this cannot supersede the

necessity of teaching him to go and thank God for all the nameless enjoyments of the day, and to ask forgiveness for the various faults he may have committed. The minds of children dwell upon particulars. They are not in habits of generalizing. It requires but little feeling to confess that we are sinners. But to specify individual acts of wickedness demands a much greater exercise of humility. And a general recognition of God's goodness affects the mind very differently from the enumeration of particular mercies. It is therefore important that your child should be taught to review the events of each day at its close. He should be reminded of the mercies received, and the faults committed; and be taught to express gratitude for the one, and implore pardon for the other. The return of a father from a journey has given your children an evening of very unusual enjoyment. When they retire for the night, allude to the happy evening they have passed. Tell them it was God who preserved their father's life, and returned him safely home. And having thus excited real gratitude in their hearts, lead them to express this gratitude in their own simple and artless language. By thus pointing their attention to prominent facts and individual blessings, they will not only acquire facility in prayer, but be most effectually taught their entire dependence upon God. Care should also be taken not to overlook the ordinary blessings of life. It is a rainy day. Show God's goodness in sending the rain. Let them see distinctly, that their Father in heaven does it that his children may have food to eat. It is night. Show them the consequences which would result if God should never again cause the sun to rise and shine upon them. They have received some needful clothes. Show them how God makes the wool grow, that they may be warm. Every mother can present innumerable such contemplations, which will enlarge their field of thought, increase their knowledge of God, promote gratitude, and give a facility in prayer which will be to them a permanent and valuable acquisition. Let it not be said that this requires a degree of knowledge and skill which but few parents possess. The chief difficulty to be surmounted is the feeling which so many parents entertain that they have not time. But the mother, who feels the importance of this subject as it deserves to be felt, will find time to be faithful with her children, whatever else she may be under the necessity of neglecting. The same course should be pursued in confession of sin. By pointing to these mercies you may easily convince your child of its want of suitable gratitude. Perhaps he has, during the day, been guilty of falsehood, or disobedience, or anger. Point to the definite case, and lead your child to confess it before God, and ask forgiveness. We will suppose that your son has been irritated, and struck his sister. Before he falls asleep, you remind him of his sin. Show him how wicked it was, and how displeased God must be. Tell him that when he is asleep he will die, unless God keeps him alive. Under such instructions, almost every child would desire to ask forgiveness, and probably would offer some such prayer as this: "O God, I am very wicked. I struck my sister. I am very sorry, and will never do so again. O God, forgive me, for Jesus Christ's sake." This would be prayer, if offered from the heart; and if, after it had been offered, the mother should kneel by the bed-side, and confess the sin of her child, and pray that God would forgive him, in all probability the intended effect of prayer would be accomplished. The offender would be penitent, and the sin forgiven. For these reasons, it is a most obvious duty to teach children to express their own feelings in their own language. And the careful mother may make this exercise one of the most efficient instruments in teaching her child obedience here, and in training it up for holiness and happiness hereafter.

Parents are apt to smile at the childish expressions which children make use of in prayer, and sometimes fear that their language is irreverent. But God looks simply at the sincerity of the petition, at its importance in the mind of the petitioner. A little child of two and a half years prayed, "Lord, help me to laugh and not to cry when mother washes me in the morning." And does not God look with as kind a regard upon the humble request of this little child, as he does upon the fervent petitions of the man who implores support under some painful operation, or strength to overcome an irritable spirit? Such a request, coming spontaneously from the heart of a child, is genuine prayer, and it shows a state of feeling which ought at all times to be cherished.

5. Expect that your child will become a Christian. That heart, which is susceptible of sorrow and of love, is capable of evangelical repentance and love to God. No one can doubt but that, at a very early period in life, a child has all the powers which are employed in the exercise of true religion. Neither can there be any doubt that at that early period the mind is more susceptible of impression, the hold of the world is more feeble, and the current of affection may be more easily turned to God. And facts do hold forth most abundant encouragement. How many little memoirs have recently been issued from the press, which have told the affecting tale of youthful piety! Children of five or six years of age have given the most gratifying evidence of attachment to the Savior. They have endured pain, and met death, sustained by the consolations of religion. Such facts have been too numerous and too decisive to allow unbelief to be longer excusable. And yet it is to be feared that many parents do not feel their immediate responsibility. They still cherish the impression that their children must attain maturity before they can be decidedly penitent for sin, and the friends of God. But the mother, who entertains such feelings as these, is guilty of the cruelest injustice to her child. It is almost impossible that she should be vigilant and faithful in her efforts, unless she expects success. Every mother ought to engage in the duties of religious instruction, with the confident expectation that God will accompany her exertions with his blessing. She ought even to feel that, if her child does not give early evidence of piety, much of the blame rests with her. The Christian experience of the child will undoubtedly differ from that of the man who has passed many years in sin, whose habits are firmly fixed, and whose affections have long been flowing in the channel of worldliness. With such a person the struggle of turning to holiness will often be great, and the sense of sin distressingly intense. But the period of your child's conversion may be at so early a stage of its existence as to leave no trace by which the time of the change can be remembered. The struggle will be comparatively feeble, and penitence will be manifested by the tearful eye and the sad heart, and not always by that deep agony of spirit which not infrequently marks the change of those who have grown old in sin.

Much injury is often done by laying stress upon the *time* when one becomes a Christian. Past feelings are at best but an uncertain test of Christian character. The great object of inquiry should be as to present feelings and conduct. Is the life now in accordance with the requirements of the Gospel? Is the heart now affected with humility, and penitence, and gratitude? Is the resolution now strong to live for God? If the sun is shining warmly upon us, it is of but little consequence at what moment it arose. There are many Christians who cannot recollect the time when they became subjects of the new birth. Be not, therefore, anxious upon this point. Indeed, by directing the attention of your child to any particular time when it became a Christian, there is danger of leading the mind to rely upon the supposed experience of that moment, rather than upon continued penitence and devotion. And therefore let every mother do all in her power to awaken in the bosoms of her children emotions of sorrow for sin, and reliance upon Christ. And when she finds these feelings in the heart, and controlling the life, let her thank God and take courage. She must watch with maternal solicitude, that temptation be avoided, and that the feeble flame burn brighter and brighter. Christ has entrusted this beloved object to your guardianship. Why should not a mother confidently expect this result to follow her efforts? Has not God encouraged her thus to hope, by promising to aid with his blessing? Has he not encouraged, by again and again crowning such efforts with success? Away then with unbelief. To doubt is to distrust the promise of God. Instruct your child, and pray for your child, and look for an immediate blessing. Thus, in all probability, will your heart be made glad by the fruits of early piety at your fire-side; grateful children will honor you through life, and the joys of heaven will be magnified by meeting your loved ones there.

6. Do not speak to others of the piety of your child. Great injury is thus often done. A child becomes deeply interested in the subject of religion, and his friends are encouraged to hope that he has really become a Christian. They speak of it to others. It is soon publicly known. He receives much attention; is caressed and flattered. Thus is this little child thrown at once into the very hottest furnace of temptation. We might refer to many painful illustrations of this truth in the memoirs of early piety.

Says the biographer of little Nathan Dickerman, "His feelings were often wounded by the injudicious conversation which was too often held in his presence. " Kind friends indulged in perhaps what were well-meant, but sadly ill-judged remarks in his presence. And it is most deeply to be regretted that parents and friends so often, inconsiderately no doubt, speak before children in praise of their persons, in a manner that inevitably fosters vanity, which injures their usefulness and happiness as long as they live.

"Nathan's ear was often greeted with, Beautiful boy! Remarkable boy! What a fine countenance! Certainly the most wonderful case I ever heard of! The half had not been told me."

It is remarkable that, while exposed to such temptations, real humility could have been preserved. And though the grace of God sustained this lovely child, but few would have escaped uninjured.

How often is even the Christian minister sensibly affected by flattery! And can a child safely receive such marked attentions? An honest development of facts, upon this subject, would be exceedingly painful. Humility is one of the cardinal virtues of Christianity. The moment an impression is conveyed to the mind that there is something remarkable and meritorious in penitence for sin, and love for God, the heart is elated with pride. And then things are said, and actions performed, to attract attention. Prayers are offered, and feelings of piety expressed, from the love of ostentation; and the child is "spoiled." Preserve your child from these temptations by giving no publicity to his feelings. Carefully cherish at home the flame which is kindled in his bosom. Under your protection, let him acquire strength of principle and stability of character. Gradually introduce him to the more public duties of the Christian life. Teach him humility. Preserve his child-like spirit. In this manner you may lead him along to be a humble, and, at the same time, an active and ardent follower of Christ.

CHAPTER EIGHT

Results

Frequent allusion has been made in the preceding chapters, to the fatal consequences which must attend the neglect of duty. In view of this, some parents may have been oppressed and dejected. It is most surely true that the misconduct of children subjects the parents to the utmost intensity of suffering. But it must be remembered, that when parental faithfulness is attended with its usual blessing, joys, nearer akin to those of heaven than of earth, are the result. The human heart is not susceptible of more exquisite pleasures than the parental relation affords. Is there no joy when the mother first presses her infant to her heart? Is there no delight in witnessing the first placid smile which plays upon its cheek? Yes! The very earliest infancy of the babe brings "rapture a mother only knows." The very care is a delight. And when your little son has passed through the dreamy existence of infancy, and is buoyant with the activity and animated with the intelligence of childhood, are not new sources of pleasure opened to your mind? Are there no thrilling emotions of enjoyment in hearing the hearty laugh of your happy boy; in witnessing the unfoldings of his active mind; in feeling his warm kiss and ardent embrace? Is there no delight in seeing your boy run to

119

meet you, with his face full of smiles and his heart full of love; and in hearing him, in lisping accents, call you mother? As you receive daily new proofs of his affection and obedience, and see that his little bosom is animated with a generous and a noble spirit, you feel repaid an hundred fold for all your pain, anxiety, and toil. After a few years your children arrive at maturity, and with that divine blessing which we may expect to accompany our prayerful efforts, they will be found with generous affections and established principles of piety. With what emotions do parents then look around upon their happy and prosperous family! They are receiving the earthly recompense of reward. What an affecting sight it is, to see an aged and widowed mother leaning upon the firm arm of her son, as he accompanies her to the house of God! And how many parents have had their declining years cheered by the affectionate attentions of a daughter! Who will so tenderly watch over you in sickness as a daughter, whose bosom is animated by the principles of piety which you have inculcated? Among the sweetest earthly joys to be experienced in old age, is the joy of looking around upon happy and grateful children. The marks of esteem and love you receive from them will daily be rewarding you for all your toil. And when your children's children cluster around you, giving unceasing tokens of respect and affection, you will find in their caresses the renewal of your youth. When all other earthly joys have faded, you will find in the little prattlers of the fire-side untiring enjoyment.

But there is a scene of still brighter happiness. The Christian family will meet again. Parents and children will be associated in heaven. And when the whole household are happily assembled there; when they sit down together in the green pastures and by the still waters; when they go in and out at the mansions which God has prepared for them; then, and not till then, will they experience the fullness of the enjoyment with which God rewards parental fidelity. How full of rapture is the thought that the whole family may meet again in the world of songs and everlasting joy, where sorrow and sighing shall for ever flee away! As from that happy state of existence you look back upon your pilgrimage on earth, you can never regret any amount of labor you have expended, any sacrifices you have made, any sufferings you have undergone, to train up your children to be with you the heirs of a glorious immortality. O there is enough, abundantly enough, to encourage every parent to unwearied exertions! As with the deep emotions of parental love, you look upon the obedient and affectionate children who surround your fireside, your thoughts may be carried away to enjoyments infinitely richer, and for ever enduring, in the world to come.

We may be called upon to follow our children to the grave. And heart-rending is such an affliction. But if we have reason to believe that they have gone to the mansions which the Savior has prepared, much of the bitterness of the affliction is taken away. They have gone home before us. They are sheltered from every storm. They are protected from every sorrow. Soaring in angelic flights, and animated with celestial joys, they are ready to welcome us when God in his own good time shall give us entrance to those happy worlds. A gentleman was once asked if he had *lost* any of his children. "No," he replied, "I have two in heaven, but have *lost* none." To a truly Christian family the death of any one of its members is but a temporary absence, and not an eternal separation.

   2. Mothers have as powerful an influence over the welfare of future generations, as all other earthly causes combined. Thus far the history of the world has been composed of the narrations of oppression and blood. War has scattered its unnumbered woes. The cry of the oppressed has unceasingly ascended to heaven. Where are we to look for the influence which shall change this scene, and fill the earth with the fruits of peace and benevolence? It is to the power of divine truth, to Christianity, as taught from a mother's lips. In a vast majority of cases the first six or seven years decide the character of the man. If the boy leaves the paternal roof uncontrolled, turbulent, and vicious, he will, in all probability, rush on in the mad career of self-indulgence. There are exceptions; but these exceptions are rare. If, on the other hand, your son goes from home accustomed to control himself, he will probably retain that habit through life. If he has been taught to make sacrifices of his own enjoyment that he may promote the happiness of those around him, it may be expected that he will continue to practice benevolence, and consequently will be respected, and useful, and happy. If he has adopted firm resolutions to be faithful in all the relations in life, he, in all probability, will be a virtuous man and an estimable citizen, and a benefactor of his race.

   When our land is filled with pious and patriotic mothers, then will it be filled with virtuous and patriotic men. The world's redeeming influence, under the blessing of the Holy Spirit, must come from a mother's lips. She, who was first in the transgression, must be yet the principal earthly instrument in the restoration. Other causes may greatly aid. Other influences must be ready to receive the mind as it comes from the mother's hand, and carry it onward in its improvement. But the mothers of our race must be the chief instruments in its redemption. This sentiment will bear examining; and the more it is examined, the more manifestly true will it appear. It is alike the dictate of philosophy and experience. The mother who is neglecting personal effort, and relying upon other influences for the formation of virtuous character in her children, will find when it is too late, that she has fatally erred. The patriot, who hopes that schools, and lyceums,[14] and the general diffusion of knowledge, will promote the good order and happiness of the community, while family government is neglected, will find that he is attempting to purify the streams which are flowing from a corrupt fountain. It is maternal influence, after all, which must be the great agent, in the hands of God, in bringing back our guilty race to duty and happiness. O that mothers could feel this responsibility as they ought! Then would the world assume a different aspect. Then should we less frequently behold unhappy families and brokenhearted parents. A new race of men would enter upon the busy scene of life, and cruelty and crime would pass away. O mothers! Reflect upon the power your Maker has placed in your hands! There is no earthly influence to be compared with yours. There is no combination of causes so powerful in promoting the happiness or the misery of our race, as the instructions of home. In a most peculiar sense God has constituted you the guardians and the controllers of the human family.

---

[14] In 1826 in Millbury, Massachusetts, Josiah Holbrook organized a program of adult education courses he called a lyceum, named after Aristotle's school in ancient Athens. The popularity of Holbrook's program spread, and five years later, the National American Lyceum was established in New York City. In the years that followed, organizations all across the country began establishing their own lyceums; by 1834, there were several thousand.

3. Perhaps some one asks, "Is there nothing for fathers to do?" There certainly is much—very much. But this treatise is prepared to impress upon the mind the duties of mothers. Yet, lest it should he inferred from what has been written that the *whole duty* of family government rests upon the mother, I would briefly remark, that no father can be excusable for releasing himself from a full share of the responsibility. A father will often make many excuses to release himself from his duty; but alas! he cannot release his children from the ruin, or himself from the woe, which his neglect occasions. It will be a poor solace to him, as he goes in shame and sorrow to the grave, to reflect that he was busily engaged in other employments while leaving his children to mature for ignominy and disgrace. What duties can be paramount to those we owe our children? A clergyman sometimes says he has so much to do, his time is so fully occupied, that he is compelled to neglect his children. And who has the first claim upon his attention, his congregation or his children? God has placed him over a congregation, and has also made him the father of a family, and which duty does God regard as most imperative? And yet not a few instances might be pointed out, in which clergymen of devoted piety and extensive usefulness, have given their whole attention to the labors of the study and public duties, and have left their unhappy children to grow up unchecked and vicious. No one can enjoy the privilege of being a father, without having duties to perform which will require time and care. And can any time be more usefully employed than that which is passed in training up a family of children, who shall remain to do good in the world long after we are silent in the grave? Can we have any influence equal to that of pious sons and daughters? Can we bequeath the world a richer legacy than the fervent piety and active usefulness of a numerous offspring? O there is no sin which reaches so far, and extends such wide-spreading desolation, as parental neglect. No father can be guiltless in retiring from these responsibilities. The first duty enjoined upon us, is to keep our *own* hearts with diligence; the second, to lead our families to God; the third, to consult for the spiritual welfare of our neighbors; the fourth, to do all in our power to evangelize the world. And yet how many Christian ministers have paralyzed their influence, destroyed their peace of mind, and broken their hearts, by neglecting the duties they owe their children.

Many of the most eminent statesmen are thus afflicted and dishonored. And the affliction must be aggravated by the consciousness that they are reaping as they have sown. I would not willingly inflict a pang upon the heart of any parent who reads these pages, but I cannot refrain from raising a warning voice, in a view of the destruction which has gone forth, and is still going forth, from the cause we are now contemplating. The temptation is very great, for men who are engaged in literary pursuits, and overwhelmed with public cares, to neglect their domestic duties. But how ruinous is this to usefulness and happiness! It is better to be a poor man, and it is better to be a humble man, than to be disgraced in life by the profligacy of those who call us father, and to have a dying pillow planted with thorns by our children's hands. Every man, whatever be his situation in life, is bound to regard the duties he owes his children as among the most sacred he has to discharge. If he neglects them, he must reap the bitter consequences.

One other remark I must here make, as it is intimately connected with a mother's duty. A father should always endeavor to teach his children to *honor* their mother. If the father does not do this, the difficulties of the mother will be vastly increased. But where harmony of design is seen to exist between the parents, authority is strengthened. There is something in loving and revering a mother, which exerts a delightful influence upon the heart; it refines and elevates the character; and is a strong safeguard against degrading vice. Boys in particular will not long respect a mother, if they see that their father does not treat her with attention. You can hardly find a dissolute young man, who has been accustomed from infancy to look to his mother with respect and love. It is in disobedience to a mother that the career of crime generally commences. The way is thus prepared for the disregard of all parental authority. And then the progress is rapid to the boldest defiance of all the laws of God and man. Many an unhappy criminal has, from the gallows, traced back his course of guilt to the early periods of childhood, when he commenced with disobedience to a mother's commands; and he has felt and acknowledged that, had he then been habituated to obey, his whole succeeding course had probably been different. It is therefore of the first importance that nothing should be omitted tending to give the mother great and unceasing influence over the minds of her children.

4. *The subject of education must be attended to with persevering study.* And yet how many parents neglect this duty! Nothing surely can be of greater importance to the parents and child, than a correct system of family government. Every mother admits her need of information. There are many valuable

books, easy of access, which will afford great assistance. A mother should consider it one of her first duties to inform herself upon this subject, as far as her means will admit. The art of influencing and guiding the youthful mind is susceptible of almost boundless improvement, and we are unfaithful to our children if we do not become familiar with the results of the experiments of others. We ought not to stumble in darkness, when light is shining around us. There are fundamental principles in operating upon the human mind, as well as in any other science. And many an anxious mother has committed error to the serious injury of her children, which she might have avoided, had she consulted the sources of information which are at every one's hand.

How great must be the affliction of that mother, who, in consequence of neglect, has been unsuccessful with her family! She looks upon her ruined sons, and reproaches herself with the just reflection, that if she had pursued a different course, they might have been her joy and blessing. Perhaps even they throw reproaches upon her, and attribute all their guilt and wretchedness to her bad government. But few more miserable men have passed through the world than Lord Byron; and he has distinctly attributed the formation of his character, and consequently all his crime and woe, to his mother's unrestrained passions, and neglect of proper government. How must such a crimination from a dissolute son, pierce the heart of a pious mother! Knowledge of duty might have been attained, but she neglected to attain it, and through inexcusable ignorance ruined her child. An affectionate mother would be overwhelmed with anguish, if she had ignorantly administered some poisonous drug, and had seen her child in consequence expiring in agony. But how much more dreadful is it to see moral ruin caused by our own criminal ignorance! Who would not rather see a son or a daughter lie down in the grave, than see them in the wretchedness and disgrace of profligacy? If we would preserve our children, we must seek information respecting our duties.

Reading, however, of itself is not sufficient. There must be the expenditure of our own thoughts, and the vigilance of personal observation. I once knew a mother who kept a constant journal of the progress of her child from his earliest infancy. She carefully noted down her more important acts of discipline, and observed the effect which her course produced upon the character of her child. With more solicitude and vigilance than the physician watches the effect of his prescriptions, did she watch the effect of her moral remedies and antidotes. His opening faculties, the developments of his affections, his constitutional temperament, his prominent foibles, were made the subject of continued deliberation. They were committed to writing. Thus was this mother gaining information more rapidly than she could possibly gain it in any other way. She was accustoming her own mind to independent investigation and thought. Every day she was gaining knowledge of the effect of different motives upon the mind. And her influence over her child was every day increasing. Now this looks like maternal fidelity. It shows that the mother feels her need of information, and is anxious to acquire it. And it shows that she is willing to make intellectual effort herself, that she may be able to discharge her duties.

Let any mother adopt such a course as this, and she must be most rapidly advancing in the knowledge of guiding the youthful mind. When her child first manifests irritation, let her write down the course she pursued to allay that irritation, and the success which attended her efforts.

I will give a specimen of what I suppose would be the general character of such a journal.

Jan. 10, 1833. Today Charles became very angry with his sister and pushed her down. As a punishment, I gave Mary an apple, and gave Charles none. But I thought Charles seemed, instead of being subdued, to be more envious and vexed with his sister.

15. Mary today treated her brother unkindly. I thought I would try a different course from that I pursued with Charles. I called them both to me and said, "Mary, God is displeased when he sees you indulging such feelings. And now how can you ask God tonight to take care of you, when you have been disobeying him today?" Having talked with her a little while in this strain, she burst into tears, and asked her brother's forgiveness. They were soon playing again as happy and affectionate as ever. Before Mary went to sleep tonight she asked God's forgiveness, and promised that she would try never to be angry again. I cannot but hope that an impression was produced upon both their minds, which will not soon be forgotten.

18. Charles today accidentally broke a valuable lamp. I fear that I unjustly blamed him. I must endeavor to have my feelings under more perfect control.

22. Mary is beginning to manifest improper fondness for dress. We have had much company lately, and many have spoken to her about her *beautiful gown*. I must dress her in such a manner that she will not attract attention.

If some such course as this is pursued with perseverance, great skill will certainly be acquired in the art of governing. The mother must, in some way, direct the energies of her own mind to this subject. She must watch the peculiarities of the dispositions of her children. She must think and experiment for herself.

After writing the above, the following communication was placed in my hand. As it was written by a mother who has long practiced upon the plan here recommended, and who, from her numerous cares, might, with more propriety than almost any other parent, claim exemption from this duty, I with great pleasure insert it. It is the testimony of successful experiment.

"Perhaps to some mothers it may at first appear impossible to carry on, with any degree of system or accuracy, any thing like a regular journal. It is true, it would at first require some effort; but if it would aid a mother in discharging her duties, where is the conscientious parent who would shrink from such an effort? There are many benefits to be expected from such a record, and it should perhaps be merely a record or notebook, that it may not encroach too much upon the time of those mothers who are obliged to devote a great proportion of their time in attending to the domestic duties of their families.

"The first benefit resulting to the mother herself would be the necessity of making some regular mental effort. A young mother, surrounded with family cares and duties, may feel at first as if she had no time for mental and intellectual labor; but ten minutes every day devoted to such a purpose, would soon convince her that her other duties are probably the better performed for such a diary. Her duties to her children certainly will not be attended to with less interest; and she is gradually fitting herself by such discipline, however trifling, to be their teacher and guide.

"The habit of keeping such memoranda also induces a mother to look with greater scrutiny into her own motives of action, into her principles of family government, and to govern her own heart and conduct, and cultivate more of a spirit which every mother needs—a spirit of prayer.

"I am confident that, would mothers do this, mutual benefit and assistance would be given to that class of society to whom we must look for much of the future happiness of the community. And many a young parent would feel her hand strengthened and her heart lightened in the cause of infant instruction.

"The plan I would suggest might be something like the following.

"1. Notice the earliest developments of temper, and give the result of simple experiments made to subdue and conquer it.

"2. Remark what things peculiarly interest your child, and describe how you improve the opportunity of giving the child a moral and religious lesson drawn from the object of interest. Show the effect and result of such an impression.

"3. Describe the course pursued to insure obedience. State the difficulties, and how overcome.

"4. Describe the course of first religious instruction, and what generally excites the strongest interest in your child's mind.

"In this way you may assist many a trembling mother in doing her duty; and the result of an experience which perhaps it costs you but a few minutes of time to throw into a suitable form on paper, will, through the pages of some religious magazine, be circulated to the farthest parts of our country, and be exerting a powerful influence on the hearts of mothers—an inestimable one on the prospects, both for time and eternity, of the rising generation."

The following is an extract from such a notebook kept by a mother, and written without any reference to its insertion here.

"Perhaps there are few dispositions which require more judicious, firm, and steady management, in a child, than that which is often ranked under obstinacy or stubbornness. There is certainly no fault, which, if neglected, or allowed to gain strength, is more likely to bring down the heart of a parent with sorrow to the grave, and to insure to the child a youth and manhood of wretchedness. It 'grows with the growth, and strengthens with the strength.' Yet I have heard more than one mother say, 'that child is very obstinate; he will have his own way, and I suppose he is too young to understand now, and frequent punishment only hardens the heart.' A child cannot be *too young to learn;* that is, as soon as a child begins to notice and watch the tones of the voice and the expression of the countenance, it is of an age to receive moral lessons. It is undoubtedly true, that in administering punishment, care should be taken to do it in such a way that it shall tend to soften and subdue the heart, not irritate it. Yet the child must be made to feel that its *spirit* must yield to paternal authority. For instance, your child is playing with some forbidden article. You tell it gently, but firmly, to put it down—it refuses. If you rise and take it by force, the child cries—it is vexed and disappointed. Instead of this, if you say, pointing to the article, 'you *must* put it down,' and it refuses, a second command in the voice of seriousness and authority will seldom fail of ensuring obedience. The child should then see an approving look or smile, and if taken up and amused by something which you are sure will interest, it will not forget the lesson, particularly if pains is taken to associate the *forbidden* thing with something which produces a sensation of pleasure. Return to it and say, 'you must not touch that, no, no,' and repeat it two or three times. Then give the child something which is not so familiar as to be worthless, and say, 'you may have this.' A child of ten or twelve months may soon be taught, in this way, distinct lessons of obedience. If it refuses to yield some slight punishment should be inflicted, which shall connect the idea of bodily suffering or inconvenience; but care should be afterwards taken to interest the child, and your countenance should evince no anger or irritability.

"A child of less than three years was often trouble-some by the unyielding disposition he manifested. He had been severely punished for his fault, though never unless the danger of omitting it made the risk to the child's future happiness very great. Once, after a very decided case of obstinacy had occurred, it became necessary to punish him. After it was over, he said he was not sorry for the fault. He had *never* been shut up in the dark, as a punishment, because with very young children the consequences are sometimes hazardous; but it was known that in this case the child was not *afraid;* and I desired to know the effect of it, in connection with religious considerations. The following experiment was tried, and the conversation is here recorded as precisely as it occurred.

"*Mother.* I am sorry you are so naughty. I must put you into a dark closet, where nobody can see you.

"*Child.* I don't want to get up and be good, (very deliberately.)

"I kept my word, saying at the same time, 'when you are a good boy, you may call me, and I will open the door; but now you must be quiet, and not touch any thing.' He remained perfectly still more than ten minutes, then knocked loudly on the door.

"M. Are you good now?

"*Ch.* Not if I come out there.

"M. What are you knocking for?

"*Ch.* I want to get out.

"M. If you are good, I will open the door; but you have been very naughty, and troubled me. Are you going to be good?

"*Ch.* No; I a'nt good and sorry—I don't want to come out.

"M. I am very sorry that my little boy is naughty. He is in the closet, where it is very dark; and mother cannot see him, but God can see him. God is displeased with you. I want my little boy to think. Can you think of God, and ask him to take care of you, while you are so cross and ill-humored?

"He was still for about a minute, and then said, in a pleasant subdued tone, 'I am good now, ma.' He came out and went to his play, as if nothing had occurred to disturb his tranquility. I have not the least doubt that this occurrence will have a strong and lasting impression, and save a mother's heart many a pang in time to come, and prevent the necessity of severe punishment."

There is an impression upon the minds of many, that skill in governing must be instinctive; that it is an original and native talent, and not to be acquired by information or thought. But look at those parents who have been most successful in family government, and they will be found to be those who have most diligently and uniformly attended to the subject. You may go into the family of some man of celebrity, in one of the learned professions, and, as you look upon his lawless children, you are perhaps discouraged. You say, if this man, with his powerful and highly cultivated mind, cannot succeed in family government, how can I expect success? But a little observation will satisfy you, that this man is giving his time and attention to other pursuits. He is neglecting his children, and they are forming precisely those characters we should expect from the influences to which they are exposed.

No course of procedure, without the blessing of God, will result in the piety of the child. But if we go on in our attempts to govern without system, or thought, or care, we shall undoubtedly reap most bitter consequences. The mother must study her duty. She must carefully observe the effect produced by her mode of discipline. There is but little advantage to be derived from books, unless we revolve their contents in our own minds. Others may suggest the most valuable ideas. But we must take those ideas and dwell upon them, and trace out their effects, and incorporate them into our minds by associating them with others of our own. We must accustom ourselves to investigation and thought. The mother, who will do this, will most certainly grow in wisdom. She will daily perceive that she is acquiring more facility in forming in her child the character she desires. And the increasing obedience and affection she will receive will be her constant reward. Care and labor is necessary in training up a family. But no other cares are rewarded with so rich a recompense; no other labors ensure such permanent and real enjoyment. You, O mothers, have immortal souls entrusted to your keeping. Their destiny is in a great degree in your hands. Your ignorance or unfaithfulness may be the means of sinking them to the world of woe. Your fidelity, by the blessing of God, may elevate them to the mansions of heaven. You and your children may soon be ranging with angel wings the realms of blest spirits, if, here, you are faithful in prayer and effort to train them up for heaven.

Other Related SGCB Titles

The Child at Home: *Living to Please God and Your Parents* by John S.C. Abbott. This is the companion volume to the book you hold in your hands. The response to *The Mother at Home* was so encouraging Abbott went to work immediately upon this sequel. We have received numerous endorsements for this book that has been buried a century.

Little Pillows and Morning Bells by Frances Ridley Havergal
This is the volume mentioned several times in this book. It is one of the finest books to read with young children at the close and the start of every day. Miss Havergal loved children and wrote in such a way that enabled them to grasp difficult concepts by use of familiar images and examples. A heart-warming little volume.

The Pastor's Daughter: *The Way of Salvation Explained to a Young Inquirer from Reminiscences of the Conversations of her Father, Rev. Edward Payson* by Louisa Payson Hopkins
This volume grants us a rare glimpse into the household of the Payson family of Portland, Maine in the early 1800's, as Edward Payson's oldest daughter recalls the patient and loving way her father led her to true conversion over a period of more than 10 years, from 4-14.

Stepping Heavenward by Elizabeth Payson Prentiss
This volume has touched and changed the lives of hundreds of thousands of women all over the world since the day it was first published in 1869. It is a favorite of such ladies as Martha Peace, Elisabeth Elliot, Susan Hunt, Joni Eareskson Tada, Kay Arthur and many, many more. Both women and men will love it!

The Young Lady's Guide: *to the Harmonious Development of Christian Character* by Harvey Newcomb
One pastor has said, *"It should be read, studied, prayed over, and put into practice by parents, young ladies, and--yes—even young men! It should be in every home, and in the library of every young lady. It is a 'companion' book for a lifetime."* We could not agree more!

Mothers of the Wise and Good by Jabez Burns is a powerful volume intended to encourage women to embrace their high calling as they look back to the powerful impact of a mother of dozens of great and godly men. We are working on a brand new edition. Due before Mother's Day.

Call us toll free at **1-877-666-9469**
E-mail us at **sgcb@charter.net**
Visit our web site at **solid-ground-books.com**

Printed in the United States
58700LVS00005B/7

9 781932 474701